Nuclear Power
and
Nuclear Weapons Proliferation

Report of the Atlantic Council's
Nuclear Fuels Policy Working Group
Volume I

Published by

The Atlantic Council of the United States

and distributed by

Westview Press
Boulder, Colorado

Library of Congress Catalog Card Number: 78-59089

ISBN 0-917258-13-4

Printed in the United States of America

Additional copies of Volume I and Volume II may be ordered,
prepaid, at $6.00 each from:

The Atlantic Council of the United States
1616 H Street, N.W.
Washington, D.C. 20006
Telephone (202) 347-9353
Cable: ATCOUN

TABLE OF CONTENTS

Volume I: The Policy Paper   Pages

VOLUME II: The Appendices

FOREWORD

The Atlantic Council of the United States has since 1961 formulated policy recommendations for action on problems and opportunities shared by North America, Western Europe, Japan, Australia and New Zealand. Given the critical long-term energy supply situation of those democratic industrialized economies, the Council has, in recent Policy Papers, addressed the issues of developing and financing alternative energy sources, including the assurance of nuclear fuel supply and the management of its use. This Policy Paper is focused on the relationship between the production of nuclear electric power and the proliferation of nuclear weapon capability.

The crux of the matter — in the US and abroad — is to provide an assured way of economically supplying nuclear energy to meet US and other nations' energy needs, without making international relations unmanageable and national acceptance of nuclear power difficult by further proliferating nuclear weapons capability. In short, the problem is to produce nuclear energy while controlling nuclear proliferation. This simple dichotomy involves a highly complex matrix of issues which have received attention over a long period of time — beginning with the post World War II proposals for controlling the technology of and access to nuclear explosive materials, the Eisenhower proposal and Atoms-for-Peace, the International Atomic Energy Agency and the development of safeguards, the Non-Proliferation Treaty and regime, the Ford and Carter concerns, and today highlighted by United States' initiatives and international interest in developing an acceptable solution to the problem.

The work of the Atlantic Council is undertaken by private citizens acting in their individual capacities, voluntarily contributing time and talent to exchange diverse, often divergent information and views, and evolving policy recommendations deemed by them to be in the national interest. Work of this nature is the backbone of the Atlantic Council's program, and this Policy Paper is a demonstration of such work. We appreciate the manner in which John Gray as Chairman, Joe Harned as Project Director, the contributing rapporteurs and the other members of the Nuclear Fuels Policy Working Group carried out their task. The names of all of the Working Group members appear on page 11. We extend our congratulations as well as our thanks to each member of the group. While the final responsibility for the views expressed is that of the Working Group, the Council is pleased to present them for public discussion and debate, which we regard as essential to the issue.

Kenneth Rush

KENNETH RUSH
Chairman
The Atlantic Council of the United States

PREFACE

In the spring of 1976, the Atlantic Council's Nuclear Fuels Policy Working Group released the first product of its activities, the report titled *Nuclear Fuels Policy*, which included the findings and recommendations of the group in regard to current and future nuclear fuels supply and use. While a number of the report's policy recommendations were adopted by the Administration or the Congress — and in some cases, both — over the course of the next two years, US policy in this field has undergone change most significantly in regard to the perceived relationship between nuclear energy supply and nuclear weapons proliferation.

Industrialized and developing countries alike have been counting on an increasing contribution from nuclear power. However, recent developments have sensitized policy makers of the United States and other nations to concerns about nuclear proliferation—by nations or by subnational groups such as terrorists.

It was in this context that the Council's Nuclear Fuels Policy Working Group was reconvened and its membership expanded in early November of 1976, to outline a second work program, complementary to the first published report, focusing on how to define the relationship between the production of nuclear electric power and the proliferation of nuclear weapon capability. The following report is the result of those efforts over the ensuing eighteen months. In addition to the continuous evolution of the Working Group's product, the first and the penultimate drafts were critically reviewed — on an informal and personal basis — by two dozen US Government officials and some sixty officials in the government and private sectors of thirty countries and the appropriate international organizations (the International Atomic Energy Agency, the International Energy Agency, the Nuclear Energy Agency of the Organization for Economic Cooperation and Development, and Euratom). The penultimate draft was also reviewed by the Working Group, leading to the preparation of this final report. The Executive Summary was then prepared by the Chairman and Project Director of the Working Group. The result of the process is presented in this policy paper, *Nuclear Power and Nuclear Weapons Proliferation*.

In completing this project, I would like to express a deep appreciation of the manner in which the members of the Working Group and our associates in the US Government and abroad have made major contributions in a far-reaching and complex analysis and search for solutions. The Working Group have been unstinting in their interest and involvement, perceptive and patient in their comments and explanations. Financial support for research and related activities of the Working Group was made available to the Atlantic Council by the Sarah Scaife Foundation, the Exxon Corporation, and the US Department of Energy. Their support does not imply their endorsement of the Working Group's conclusions and recommendations. Support for the overall Atlantic Council program, of which this effort is a part, has been made available by a number of US foundations, corporations, labor unions and individuals. We are most grateful for this institutional support, as well as for the extraordinary contributions of time and talent by the Working Group members.

JOHN E. GRAY
Chairman
Nuclear Fuels Policy Working Group
The Atlantic Council of the United States

NUCLEAR FUELS POLICY WORKING GROUP

Chairman:

John E. Gray, President, International Energy Associates, Ltd.; Director, Atlantic Council.

Project Director:

Joseph W. Harned, Deputy Director General, Atlantic Council; US Representative, Atlantic Institute for International Affairs (Paris).

Contributing Rapporteurs:

Bernard H. Cherry, Vice President, Corporate Planning, GPU Service Corporation.

Warren H. Donnelly, Senior Specialist, Energy, Congressional Research Service, Library of Congress.

Curt Gasteyger, Director, Arms Control and International Security Program, Graduate Institute for International Studies (Geneva).

Lincoln Gordon, Senior Fellow, Resources for the Future; Former Assistant Secretary of State, Ambassador to Brazil, and President, Johns Hopkins University; Director, Atlantic Council.

Ryukichi Imai, General Manager, Engineering, Japan Atomic Power Co.; Assistant to the Chairman, Japan Enrichment and Reprocessing Group; member of the Standing Advisory Group on Safeguards Implementation, International Atomic Energy Agency.

Myron B. Kratzer, Senior Consultant, International Energy Associates, Ltd.; Former Deputy Assistant Secretary of State.

L. Manning Muntzing, Partner, Doub, Purcell, Muntzing & Hansen; Former Director of Regulation, Atomic Energy Commission.

John G. Palfrey, Guest Scholar, Brookings Institution; Professor of Law, Columbia University; Former Commissioner, Atomic Energy Commission.

Margaret Paradis, Attorney, LeBoeuf, Lamb, Leiby & MacRae.

11

Members:

Frank Barnaby, Director, Stockholm International Peace Research Institute (Stockholm).

W. Donham Crawford, President, Edison Electric Institute. (Alternate: Justin Karp, Vice President, EEI).

Raymond L. Dickeman, President, Exxon Nuclear Company.

George Driscoll, International Economist.

Robert F. Ellsworth, Former Deputy Secretary of Defense and Ambassador to NATO; Director, Atlantic Council.

William C. Foster, Chairman, Arms Control Association; Former Director, Arms Control and Disarmament Agency; Former Deputy Secretary of Defense; Director, Atlantic Council.

Richard L. Garwin, IBM Fellow, Thomas J. Watson Research Center; Former Member, Defense Science Board and President's Science Advisory Committee.

Andrew J. Goodpaster, Superintendent, United States Military Academy; Former Supreme Allied Commander, Europe; Vice Chairman, Atlantic Council.

Michael Goppel, First Secretary, Delegation of the Commission of the European Communities to the US.

John N. Irwin II, Attorney, Patterson, Belknap & Webb; Former Assistant Secretary of Defense, Deputy Secretary of State and Ambassador to France; Director, Atlantic Council.

Henry D. Jacoby, Professor of Economics, Sloan School of Management, Massachusetts Institute of Technology.

W. Robert Keagy, International Energy Consultant (Zurich).

Robert Kleiman, Editorial Board, *The New York Times.*

John M. Leddy, Former Assistant Secretary of State and the Treasury; Former Ambassador to the OECD; Director, Atlantic Council.

David E. Lilienthal, Chairman, Development and Resources Corporation; Former Chairman, Atomic Energy Commission.

Harald B. Malmgren, President, Malmgren Inc.; Former Ambassador and Deputy Special Representative for Trade Negotiations; Director, Atlantic Council.

R. Eric Miller, Vice President, Bechtel Corporation. (Alternate: Ken Davis, Bechtel Power).

Laurence I. Moss, Consultant on Energy/Environment; Former President, Sierra Club.

Paul H. Nitze, Consultant; Former Delegate to SALT; Former Deputy Secretary of Defense and Secretary of the Navy; Director, Atlantic Council.

Hilliard W. Paige, Director and Senior Consultant, International Energy Associates, Ltd.; Former President, General Dynamics Corporation.

Jean-Pierre Poullier, International Economist (Paris).

Norman C. Rasmussen, Professor of Nuclear Engineering, Massachusetts Institute of Technology.

John C. Sawhill, President, New York University; Former Administrator, Federal Energy Office.

Thomas C. Schelling, Lucius N. Littauer Professor of Political Economy, JFK School of Government, Harvard University.

Chauncey Starr, President, Electric Power Research Institute. (Alternate: Robert Loftness, Division Director, EPRI Washington).

Julian J. Steyn, Senior Consultant, International Energy Associates Ltd.; Former Vice President, NUS Corporation.

Mason Willrich, Director, International Relations Division, Rockefeller Foundation; Former Assistant General Counsel, Arms Control and Disarmament Agency.

Ex-Officio Members:

Theodore C. Achilles, Vice Chairman, Atlantic Council; Former Counselor of the State Department and Ambassador to Peru.

W. Randolph Burgess, Vice Chairman, Atlantic Council; Former Under Secretary of the Treasury and Ambassador to NATO and the OEEC.

Francis O. Wilcox, Director General, Atlantic Council; Former: Assistant Secretary of State; Chief of Staff, Senate Foreign Relations Committee; Dean, School of Advanced International Studies, Johns Hopkins University.

Project Assistant:

Eliane Lomax, Staff Member, Atlantic Council.

EXECUTIVE SUMMARY

I. INTRODUCTION

The purpose of this policy paper is to recommend actions that will help to keep within acceptable bounds the risks of the further spread or proliferation of nuclear weapons, while meeting the needs of nations for nuclear energy. The problems associated with nuclear proliferation risks — like those associated with nuclear energy supply and use — lie beyond the domain of any one nation, and therefore require a coordinated combination of national and cooperative international measures.

The relationship between peaceful nuclear power and nuclear weapons proliferation is explored here to assess its nature, to examine the factors which affect the degree of proliferation risk posed by the use of nuclear power throughout the world, and to compare this risk with risks of proliferation independent of nuclear power.

As documented in the Atlantic Council's earlier report, *Nuclear Fuels Policy,* nuclear power is viewed by many nations as a vital energy source required to help meet present and future energy needs. Leading industrial states have proceeded with national nuclear energy programs based upon express commitments in the Non-Proliferation Treaty and fundamental assurances from nuclear supplier states, in particular the US, that they would be supplied nuclear technology, equipment and materials on a reliable and non-discriminatory basis. Events in recent years, epitomized by the 1973 OAPEC oil embargo, have heightened many nations' concern with their energy needs and supply, and therefore have increased interest in nuclear power as a partial substitute for imported oil. With critical shortages of oil anticipated later in this century, non-proliferation objectives cannot be achieved by limiting world use of nuclear power, even were it desirable and possible.

The relevance of nuclear power programs to proliferation risk arises mainly from the possibility that the potential access these programs may provide to weapon-usable fissile material may influence either the decision to seek nuclear weapons or the ability to implement such a decision. Until recently, it was the general presumption by both supplier and recipient states that cooperation in sharing the benefits of peaceful nuclear energy would continue beyond light water reactor technology, ultimately to include reprocessing and entry into the plutonium fuel cycle. If that presumption is to be changed, there is a need to create a new understanding among nations on non-proliferation goals and means of achieving them in a manner compatible with long-term economic supply of electricity generated with nuclear power. Therefore, this Atlantic Council study considers the actions needed to contain proliferation risks from all phases of the nuclear power fuel cycle.

Important as it is in its own right, the issue of terrorism and other forms of *sub*national diversion or theft of nuclear material are not defined as proliferation as that term is used in this report. The distinction is not an artificial or formal one. Terrorist threats to nuclear material are of a different nature and

15

are susceptible to very different forms of protection than are the risks of governmental diversion and national proliferation. Moreover, governments possess both resources and virtually unlimited authority, including police power, to counter subnational threats, while the risks of national diversion must be dealt with through the relatively limited tools of diplomacy, international institutions, and sanctions. While the problem of terrorism and physical security is properly receiving continuing attention, the risk of nations proliferating is increasingly being recognized as the greater and perhaps more intractable risk.

Developments in the past few years have dramatized many issues surrounding nuclear power. In particular, the new initiatives and constraints proposed by Presidents Ford and Carter and by the US Congress, which re-emphasize the earlier recognized linkages between certain aspects of nuclear power and proliferation, make it important that the relationship between nuclear power development and nuclear weapons capabilities be clearly understood both in historical perspective and in current terms.

II. THE MANAGEMENT OF PROLIFERATION

The central principle of the Non-Proliferation Treaty (NPT) and the International Atomic Energy Agency (IAEA) has been the concept of international cooperation in peaceful nuclear development, mainly for electric power supply, in return for a forswearing by non-weapon states of weapons acquisition, and acceptance by them of international safeguards. This concept inherently entails discrimination between nuclear weapon states and non-weapon states. To be acceptable, a non-proliferation policy based on international cooperation for peaceful development should come as close as possible to symmetry and non-discrimination in nuclear energy development. Only in this way can institutional arrangements for nuclear fuel cycle options which offer increased proliferation resistance effectively take account of the interests and sensitivities of the less-developed countries. There should be no *a priori* judgment that a permanent class of "third world" countries has no need for nuclear energy. The aim should be identical treatment for all non-weapon states willing to forswear explosive devices and accept international full-scope safeguards. It should be recognized that the most likely candidates for proliferation may well be those developing countries that are already substantially industrialized. Development of a cooperative approach to non-proliferation requires the participation of all states with a serious interest in nuclear energy development, rather than confrontation between a supplier group and recipients.

While an approach focusing on the individual situation of each of some 10 or 20 current weapon threshold countries can prove successful, it can do so only in the short term, for additional countries are bound to arrive at that same threshold in the course of their economic and technological development. In other words, there must be a distinction made between two kinds of proliferation. The first kind is a country-specific scenario of nations close to weapon capability now: the near-term proliferation problem. It is this problem that must be dealt with on a case-by-case basis. The second kind of proliferation, the longer-term problem, relates to the worldwide advancement in nuclear and other industrial technologies: a more general and abstract problem, but nonetheless real.

The country-specific, near-term proliferation problem must be addressed through export policies, sanctions, supply security and regional security guarantees and other measures that involve incentives and disincentives tailored to individual nations' perceived needs. The more general, longer-term proliferation threat is evidently what the Carter Administration policy makers have in mind in re-evaluating alternative fuel cycles and attempting to control the role of plutonium in future nuclear power. The most difficult aspect of this approach is that it is discriminatory: the problem becomes one of defining those "qualified" (for using plutonium) without antagonizing others.

III. ALTERNATIVE ROUTES TO NUCLEAR WEAPONS

Because uranium enrichment provides a direct route to the production of weapon-usable material, and because the technology development for its large-scale production was viewed as an especially difficult accomplishment, a certain mystique has always been associated with enrichment, and certain aspects of the technology remain classified to the present day. Nevertheless, it is an oversimplification to assume that all uranium enrichment technology is classified, or that it presents difficulties which make its development by additional nations highly improbable.

Gaseous diffusion enrichment remains the process by which the overwhelming proportion of enriched uranium is produced at present. The United States, United Kingdom, Soviet Union, France and China have all constructed and operate gaseous diffusion plants. These plants are capable of — and have been — producing both weapon-grade and power reactor-grade enriched uranium.

The centrifuge enrichment process is regarded by some as representing a high proliferation risk due to its small size and low power requirements, characteristics which could facilitate clandestine operation. Some observers believe that a moderately industrialized country can successfully build and operate small centrifuge enrichment plants relying on information available in the open literature. These plants would not be economical for nuclear power purposes, but could produce significant quantities of weapon-grade material at moderate cost. The "safeguardability" of commercial-sized centrifuge plants, built on an economic scale, is considerably better.

Laser enrichment technology, which if successful would allow the production of significant amounts of enriched material in extremely compact facilities, is a source of some concern to all who are involved with nonproliferation. But it is simply too early to forecast, at least on the basis of information in the public domain, whether this technology, if it proves to be viable, will be available to or reproducible by less sophisticated countries.

A very different direct route to nuclear weapons, taken by the nuclear-weapon states in the past, has been the construction of ''plutonium production'' reactors to provide the explosive material. These are essentially natural uranium ''production'' or even ''research'' reactors, versions of which have long existed throughout the world using widely known technology.

In contrast to production or research reactors, clandestine diversion of material for nuclear weapons purposes from civilian nuclear power facilities is difficult, and involves a substantial risk of detection. As nations come to rely more on power reactors to meet their growing energy needs, the incentives to cheat on safeguards decrease rapidly with their increasing vulnerability to sanctions on supplies by the world nuclear community.

However, in pursuing the nuclear power route, a nation can build up a large inventory of plutonium-bearing spent fuel. If it acquires a reprocessing plant for the purpose of plutonium recycle, it is provided with an overt way to build up a stockpile of separated plutonium. Plutonium separation has come to be regarded as a basic point of connection between nuclear power and nuclear weapon capabilities. The new US position seeks to keep these activities as separate as possible. However, once countries engage in reprocessing and plutonium recycle, for light water reactors or breeder reactors, or both, the line between nuclear power and nuclear weapons is no longer the presence of and national access to separated plutonium but the use of the separated plutonium in a reactor or in an explosive device.

If stockpiles of plutonium accumulate in national hands, international safeguards as a means of detecting diversion, and therefore of deterring it by providing advance warning, become less meaningful. Even if safeguards work perfectly, the warning signal would come only when the plutonium is taken from the stockpile, presumably for insertion into a pre-constructed explosive device.

What is at issue is not simply the question of whether sensitive activities, such as plutonium recycle and accumulation, can take place with adequate assurance against proliferation, but how peaceful nuclear activities are to proceed without unacceptable proliferation risks, given the accessibility of reprocessing technology and the ability of moderately industrialized nations to build workable reprocessing facilities.

IV. INSTITUTIONAL INNOVATIONS AND NON-PROLIFERATION

The knowledge, technical capacity, and basic materials for making nuclear explosives are by now widespread in the world. International cooperation is therefore indispensable to policies aimed at minimizing the extent and delaying the timing of any further proliferation. Such policies must seek to influence potential proliferators in two respects: reducing their *motivation* for securing nuclear weapons and impeding their access to *means* for doing so.

Any practical set of policies will have to include some constraints and some affirmative cooperation. The broad policy orientation will probably be a judicious mix of the historical reliance on denial and sanctions organized by the "haves" against the "have-nots", and the newly evolving reliance on a proliferation-resistant regime organized cooperatively among all nations with a serious and responsible interest in nuclear power development.

The report reaffirms the utility of the earlier policy orientation, but looks to new forms of international cooperation, including institutional innovations, as the most promising means of strengthening its effectiveness in limiting proliferation. There is strong evidence that a political consensus opposing proliferation is very widely shared among both industrial and developing non-weapon states. Institutional innovations can reinforce that consensus in four ways: (a) by improving the security and economy of fuel supply and the access to the benefits of technological improvements as they are developed; (b) by minimizing the degree of discrimination among different classes of countries; (c) by reducing the motivation for weapons acquisition arising from regional rivalries, the desire to pre-empt suspicious neighbors, or supposed prestige; and (d) by reducing the access to means for proliferation through appropriate multinational control.

If they are to prove to be broadly acceptable and effective, such measures to control the proliferation of nuclear weapons capabilities should be balanced by obligations to control the growth and sophistication of current nuclear arsenals. The US has therefore embarked on negotiations with the United Kingdom and the Soviet Union, on a multilateral, comprehensive nuclear test ban. The goal of such a comprehensive test ban is to halt completely any testing which serves to advance nuclear weapon development anywhere in the world. It would impose limitations on nuclear weapon states and non-nuclear weapon states alike, and could contribute in a substantial way to reducing incentives for non-nuclear weapon states to pursue development of the technology leading to a nuclear explosive.

V. CONCLUSIONS

The US has not had effective world control over "sensitive nuclear technology" for a long time. Nor does the US have effective control over world uranium resources — either for purposes of supply or denial. There have been recurring demonstrations of the ability of others to enrich uranium and to produce plutonium. This includes a number of non-weapon states. Consequently, while the US has some ability to unilaterally influence the risk of nuclear proliferation, this is limited.

Just as there is no unilateral solution which the US can impose, neither is there a technological panacea, a "technical fix" which could be applied to enrichment, reprocessing and recycle, and to the breeder fuel cycle, to sever their potential link with proliferation. On the other hand, it is both possible and practical to seek out technical measures which *might* make it more difficult for nations to divert nuclear materials from peaceful uses towards nuclear weapons and *would* strongly inhibit access to fissile material by *sub*national groups. Though it is not technically feasible to prevent national diversion of special nuclear material and facilities, technology can and should continue to be developed which would further reduce the possibility of theft by terrorists.

The prevention of proliferation will not be assured by unilaterally developing alternative fuel cycles or delaying reprocessing or the breeder reactor. The potential for further proliferation is both immediate and diffuse — for there are over 200 power reactors and at least as many research reactors around the world producing plutonium today. Breeder reactors are simply another potential source of plutonium, whose use requires reprocessing. Decisions concerning the use of breeders therefore determine the absolute answer as to whether or not reprocessing is necessary. In the meantime, literally hundreds of conventional reactors are in place and operating, with their attendant spent fuel problems.

An effective non-proliferation strategy calls for unusual cooperation within the interdependent world community. If the US can forego the temptation of unilateral action, US influence and concern about proliferation can have a major effect. However, for this influence to be effective, it is important to counter supplier and recipient suspicions that the new US concern with non-proliferation — focusing upon avoidance of reprocessing and the plutonium economy — is due as much to its own economic interest as to the more important problem of world security.

A related difficulty is that the US Federal Government remains poorly equipped to deal with important issues that combine both foreign and domestic elements. Energy policy and natural resources policy are beset by foreign supply considerations, domestic constituencies, and fragmentation of authority among the 50 states. The isolation of domestic from foreign affairs may have been tolerable in simpler times. Now, policies for energy, nuclear power, non-proliferation and natural resources demand integration of foreign and domestic considerations.

For the greatest effect, US efforts should be focused through an international dialogue with supplier and recipient states. It may still be possible for the supplier states, for a limited time, to exact assurances of non-proliferation from recipient states. However, this leverage will be short-lived. There is little time — but absolute need — for US non-proliferation policy to be coordinated with other aspects of foreign policy, and in particular with defense and economic issues. Furthermore, non-proliferation policy must attempt to provide the countries using nuclear energy with solid reasons not to receive or develop sensitive nuclear materials or facilities. Recipient states, therefore, must be consulted and listened to during the policy formulation process, with particular emphasis on the assurance of nuclear fuel supply security.

In order to be effective, nuclear fuel supply security would have to be both economic and credible. While US policy makers would probably be willing to pay a "non-proliferation premium" by providing an assured economic supply internationally, the US would be binding itself to a commitment which would appear to be vulnerable to the vagaries of its political process and to competition with domestic nuclear fuel needs. A more attractive and effective option would be US commitment to one or more multinational nuclear fuel supply sources. National decisions concerning reprocessing and the breeder reactor will eventually affect the amount of high-level waste disposal and spent fuel storage needs, but cannot alter the fact that they are needed now and on an increasing scale that cannot be met by individual countries acting alone. The logical starting point is, therefore, to organize multinational facilities which can meet the spent fuel storage need, and which can evolve to meet other fuel cycle supply needs as and when those functions are incorporated in the multinational system. Nuclear waste management could be provided on a multinational basis as an incentive to those countries willing to place national reprocessing facilities under international control in a multinational nuclear fuel supply system.

The International Nuclear Fuel Cycle Evaluation (INFCE) affords the world community an unusual opportunity to explore alternative fuel cycles from the perspective of the most knowledgeable supplier and recipient states. Some current non-proliferation hopes appear to rely too heavily on unproven technical approaches. Evaluation of the benefits and feasibility of these technical approaches should take place in the course of INFCE. As the evaluation allows a dialogue among supplier and user states, a record should emerge which will serve as a useful reference for all states in nuclear energy planning.

If action were taken to meet the perceived need of supplying spent fuel storage and/or high-level waste management, it would appear that a parallel step may be taken to meet the perceived threat of the proliferation of national enrichment and reprocessing facilities. One recommended approach has been for the US and other existing suppliers to implement a policy to assure the provision of enrichment services at the lowest possible cost. The complementary step that could provide an alternative to national reprocessing facilities is multinational nuclear fuel supply services and their international control and safeguards.

The more national adherents these multinational measures gain, the greater will be their legitimacy and supply credibility — and the more difficult it will be for individual countries to remain outside this solution, retaining sensitive national facilities. The opportunity exists for the US, working cooperatively with the European Community, Japan and others, to organize a multinational nuclear fuel cycle supply system in which other nations participate as founders and users — and as producers when appropriate.

As envisioned, such a system would be as (or more) proliferation-resistant than the dispersed, once-through fuel cycle with indefinite spent fuel storage. Other nations may support such a system only if it includes the technical and economic capabilities of the US and other industrialized nuclear power states, and clearly provides for participation by other states in roles commensurate with their evolving economic and energy interests and capabilities.

The opportunity for bringing about productive innovations would appear to be enhanced by: (1) making maximum use of existing national facilities and institutions, private and public; (2) expanding from such a base on a pragmatic and controlled basis; and (3) keeping to the necessary minimum of size and complexity, and maximum of speed and effectiveness, the international system required to control, inspect and audit access to sensitive materials.

Working out detailed arrangements for multinational operating institutions is likely to be easier than securing the domestic and international political consensus for their establishment. This will require a convincing demonstration to countries in a variety of political, geographical, resource, and developmental conditions that a multinational nuclear supply system is the superior option for each of them compared with realistic alternatives—superior in terms of both reliable and economic energy supply and national security.

The following recommendations support the goal of meeting nuclear energy supply requirements while optimizing safeguards against nuclear proliferation.

VI. RECOMMENDATIONS

As a matter of course, the United States and other industrialized countries should adopt and implement comprehensive, long-term energy policies aimed at reducing, by strict energy conservation measures and by maximum development of alternate energy sources and resources, their dependence on imported petroleum. The US could and should take the lead. This action would help to alleviate pressures on the world petroleum market, to stabilize petroleum prices, and to contribute to making the diminishing world petroleum reserves available, under acceptable conditions, to others, particularly to the less developed countries.

In implementing non-proliferation policy, the US government should first acknowledge the validity of its existing agreements for cooperation, subsequent arrangements and contracts concerning nuclear supply, and in that context, and in a spirit of partnership, proceed to negotiate further desired conditions of supply for nuclear exports. The US should tailor its approach to non-nuclear weapon states to help meet their specific needs—political and security as well as economic—so as to offset the pressures for national nuclear weapon capability. US policy should reflect the distinction between the near-term, country-specific proliferation threat of nations close to weapon capability now, and the longer-term threat of additional countries approaching the same threshold in the course of their further economic and technological development. The US should take a case-by-case approach in forestalling countries close to proliferation. For countries further from proliferation, the US approach should try to encourage them to join the US in forming a system which will preclude their need to produce sensitive nuclear materials nationally. By facilitating the transfer of non-sensitive nuclear materials and technologies, the US should demonstrate that adherents to the NPT, and others accepting full-scope safeguards, can enjoy the benefits of nuclear power without possession and use of sensitive nuclear materials and technologies.

The US should promptly make domestic and multilateral arrangements to provide a credible assured nuclear fuel supply to states desiring to develop nuclear power which are adherents to the NPT or otherwise accept full-scope safeguards. Supplier and recipient states should jointly ensure that multinational spent nuclear fuel storage facilities are operative and adequate to meet their needs by 1985 at the latest. These facilities should be planned so that they can be built in stages, leaving open the possibility of eventually co-locating with them other fuel cycle facilities. Specifically, high level radioactive waste management should be provided on a multinational basis as an incentive to those countries willing to place national reprocessing facilities under international control in the multinational nuclear fuel supply system described in the following recommendation.

In implementing the recommendations above, the United States cooperatively with other willing nations should develop a multinational system with the following purposes: (a) carrying out economically and safely the necessary nuclear fuel supply functions; and (b) providing practical political, physical and technical safeguards against diversion of fissile materials and production facilities. This action could be initiated in conjunction with or separate from INFCE. Consideration should be given to forging a multinational nuclear fuel supply system which would utilize existing national facilities as the base for creating a broadly based institution which would enhance the security of nuclear fuels supply, and which would under international supervision safeguard these same sensitive fuel cycle facilities and materials. In this context the availability of an adequately safeguarded international transport system for special nuclear materials should be assured promptly by the supplier and recipient nations, with immediate emphasis on spent fuel transport.

The US should develop and demonstrate proliferation-resistant breeder technology in regard to reactors, fuel preparation and use, storage and transportation, reprocessing and radioactive waste management. In doing so, the US should create a positive basis for close cooperation with other nations on breeders with the intent to provide strong technological as well as political leadership internationally on developing and demonstrating proliferation-resistant technology and institutions, as well as on later deployment decisions. Plutonium-fueled breeders should be included.

The continued vital role of the IAEA in the application of safeguards should be assured as a fundamental element in any non-proliferation policy. In general, IAEA member states' fuel cycle facilities — including new US enrichment capacity — should be constructed and organized to permit maximum effectiveness of inspection and accountability of material flows, and improved reliability, standardization, accuracy and quality of safeguards measurements. In particular, the US should promptly implement the safeguards agreement with the IAEA which was proposed by the US more than ten years ago, and continue to press for effective safeguards, both domestically and internationally. Prompt attention should be directed toward the development of safeguards for the new enrichment technologies as well as for reprocessing.

The US should continue to press for universal adherence to the Non-Proliferation Treaty. Until such time as that goal is achieved, the US should foster a common front among all nuclear supplier and recipient countries to the effect that further shipments of nuclear fuel and equipment require full-scope safeguards on all nuclear facilities, acquired or indigenous, in the recipient country. Moreover, the US and other governments interested in the further development of nuclear power should promptly pool information, share technical and institutional measures and where appropriate take concerted action which can prevent the theft or diversion of sensitive nuclear materials and facilities by terrorists and other subnational groups.

The US should provide — both unilaterally and multilaterally through a cooperative international regime — appropriate sanctions for any nation which chooses to violate non-proliferation commitments or safeguard agreements. The cooperative international regime would consist of supply sanctions extended by suppliers' agreement embracing all nuclear facilities of countries receiving any outside assistance of supply of fuel, facilities, or know-how. The US should take the lead in creating an international agreement or code of conduct to provide flexible early-warning and response to nuclear misconduct, complementing the more formal IAEA-NPT procedures and developing further the London Nuclear Suppliers' Group Guidelines. Specifically, this new agreement could, if necessary, trigger appropriate cooperative as well as unilateral sanctions. As well, the agreement should provide a forum for arbitration of national instances and complaints of misconduct. But the primary purpose of the initiative must remain to treat national violations with the utmost speed in the most severe manner possible.

INFCE should have as a primary goal a thorough, balanced and objective analysis of the advantages and disadvantages of each nuclear fuel cycle with reference to economics, non-proliferation and other factors. INFCE should supplement on-going national and multinational R&D programs concerning the fuel cycle. The results of these on-going activities would be a useful and timely contribution to INFCE, while preventing strategic slippage in R&D during the course of the international evaluation.

Finally, in order to reinforce international acceptance of the foregoing recommendations concerning measures to reduce the likelihood and extent of nuclear proliferation, the US, the Soviet Union, and other nuclear weapon and non-nuclear weapon states should urgently establish a comprehensive nuclear weapon test ban intended to contribute in a substantial way to reducing incentives for present non-nuclear weapon states to pursue development of technology leading to a nuclear explosive capability.

Nuclear Power
and
Nuclear Weapons Proliferation

I. INTRODUCTION TO THE ISSUES

The purpose of this policy paper is to recommend actions that will help to keep within acceptable bounds the risks of the further spread or proliferation of nuclear weapons, while meeting the needs of nations for nuclear energy. The problems associated with nuclear proliferation risks — like those associated with nuclear energy supply and use[1] — lie beyond the domain of any one nation, and therefore require a coordinated combination of national and cooperative international measures.

The relationship between peaceful nuclear power and nuclear weapons proliferation is explored here to assess its nature, to examine the factors which affect the degree of proliferation risk posed by the use of nuclear power throughout the world, and to compare this risk with risks of proliferation independent of nuclear power.

Nuclear power is viewed by many nations as a vital energy source required to help meet present and future energy needs. Leading industrial states have proceeded with national nuclear energy programs based upon express commitments in the Non-Proliferation Treaty and fundamental assurances from nuclear supplier states, in particular the US, that they would be supplied nuclear technology, equipment and materials on a reliable and non-discriminatory basis. Events in recent years, epitomized by the 1973 OAPEC oil embargo, have heightened many nations' concern with their energy needs and suppliers, and therefore have increased interest in nuclear power as a partial substitute for imported oil. With critical shortages of oil anticipated later in this century, non-proliferation objectives cannot be achieved solely by limiting world use of nuclear power, even were it desirable and possible, given the present economic and political perspectives of these states.

Other recent events, in particular the 1974 nuclear explosion in India, however, have created considerable controversy and confusion as to the

---

[1]See the Working Group's earlier report on current and future nuclear fuel supply and use: *Nuclear Fuels Policy,* The Atlantic Council of the United States, Washington, D.C., 1976.

adequacy of existing policies to forestall additional nations from acquiring nuclear weapons, particularly those planning intensive use of nuclear energy. The urgent tenor of the non-proliferation debate in the US has created a push for a rapid and secure solution to the non-proliferation problem. Certain parts of some nuclear power fuel cycles have become the focus of concern of those who fear proliferation potential of nuclear power technology, equipment and material.

The evolving history of US non-proliferation policy began a new chapter on March 10, 1978, when President Carter signed into law the Non-Proliferation Act of 1978 (Public Law 95-242). In signing this Act of Congress, the President committed the United States to three major, simultaneous international negotiations, and to three more substantial international cooperative efforts, all intended to keep within acceptable limits any increased risks of proliferation from increased world use of nuclear power. The three negotiations mandated in the Act are to:

- develop international approaches to meeting future world nuclear needs, including establishment of an interim international stockpile of slightly enriched uranium and, ultimately, establishment of an international nuclear fuel authority to supply nuclear fuel to nations that adhere to certain non-proliferation commitments;

- renegotiate all existing agreements for nuclear cooperation with other nations and international organizations; and

- seek agreement with other nations, or groups of nations, to adhere to certain policies for control of nuclear exports.

As for US cooperative initiatives, the Act requires the US to:

- seek to act with other nations to strengthen the International Atomic Energy Agency (IAEA) and its safeguards;

- negotiate with other nations, and groups of nations, to establish sanctions for violation of the Non-Proliferation Treaty (NPT) principles by nations and to deal with theft or diversion of nuclear materials by any person or group; and

- cooperate with other nations and organizations to assist in developing non-nuclear energy resources to aid developing countries in meeting their energy needs, and to help developing and industrialized nations in protecting the environment from effects associated with the use of nuclear power.

The course of these international initiatives will be influenced by perceptions in the US and other nations of the nature and severity of the risks of further proliferation and the efficacy of various preventive measures. The Nuclear Fuels Policy Working Group of the Atlantic Council hopes in this report to contribute to public understanding of the issues involved. The Working Group also hopes to provide those representing the US and other nations in the negotiations with a fresh look at these issues. In many instances, the Working Group's analysis runs parallel to that of President Carter and his administration. In some instances, it diverges.

The relevance of nuclear power programs to proliferation risk arises mainly from the possibility that the potential access these programs may provide to weapon-usable fissile material may influence either the decision to seek nuclear weapons or the ability to implement such a decision. Until recently, it was the general presumption by both supplier and recipient states that cooperation in sharing the benefits of peaceful nuclear energy would continue beyond light water reactor technology, ultimately to include reprocessing and entry into the plutonium fuel cycle. If that presumption is now to be changed, then there is a need to create a new understanding among nations on non-proliferation goals and means of achieving them in a manner compatible with long-term economic supply of electricity generated with nuclear power. Therefore, this Atlantic Council study considers the actions needed to contain proliferation risks from all phases of the nuclear power fuel cycle.

Important as it is in its own right, the issue of terrorism and other forms of *sub*national diversion or theft of nuclear material are usually not defined as proliferation as that term is used in this report. The distinction is not an artificial or formal one. Terrorist threats to divert nuclear material are of a different nature and are susceptible to very different forms of protection than are the risks of governmental diversion and national proliferation. Moreover, governments possess both resources and virtually unlimited authority, including police power, to counter subnational threats, while the risks of national diversion must be dealt with through the relatively limited tools of diplomacy, international institutions, and sanctions. While the problem of terrorism and physical security is properly receiving continuing attention, the risk of proliferation in the traditional sense is increasingly being recognized as the greater and perhaps more intractable risk.

Developments in the past few years have dramatized many issues surrounding nuclear power. In particular, the new initiatives and constraints proposed by Presidents Ford and Carter and by the US Congress, which re-emphasize the earlier recognized linkages between certain aspects of nuclear power and proliferation, make it important that the relationship between nuclear power development and nuclear weapons capabilities be clearly understood both in historical perspective and in current terms.

A. The 1970s: New Developments and Challenges

The early 1970s were a period of comparative complacency. After the Non-Proliferation Treaty (NPT) was successfully negotiated in 1968 and entered into force in 1970, the number of NPT member states steadily increased, and ultimately included the membership of the most advanced non-nuclear weapon states. The NPT formally committed non-nuclear weapon states not to build nuclear weapons or peaceful nuclear explosives, and to accept mandatory international safeguards on all their peaceful nuclear facilities. Following the test of a nuclear explosion by the People's Republic of China in 1964, which raised the number of nuclear weapon states to five, no additional nation demonstrated a nuclear explosive device until India's test ten years later in May 1974. The dangers of an increase in the number of nuclear weapon countries came to the forefront of public attention in 1973-74 with three developments.

The surging price of oil accompanying the OAPEC embargo of 1973, and OPEC's successful control of the oil market, confirmed for many advanced and developing countries that they should continue the development of nuclear power. The second development, India's nuclear explosion of May 1974, demonstrated that any country having unsafeguarded spent fuel, and capable of constructing a small reprocessing plant to recover plutonium can probably develop a nuclear explosive. (It should be noted that India has never been party to the Non-Proliferation Treaty.)

The third development of the 1970s was the rapid maturing of nuclear power in the advanced countries, particularly in Western Europe and Japan, and the parallel development of credible and competitive industries for the supply of power reactors, reactor components, and other nuclear facilities. There were disturbing indications that the principal suppliers, in seeking competitive advantage at times when new orders were few and far between, might offer less demanding non-proliferation conditions to purchasers. In addition, a new tactic was exhibited by at least one supplier, West Germany. West Germany agreed to tie the sale of several nuclear power plants (the most profitable component for its nuclear industry) to the sale of other nuclear equipment, particularly enrichment and reprocessing plants. Such a package would inevitably provide the reactor purchaser with the capability to separate plutonium, and at a minimum would also provide fuel stocks which after further enrichment would be usable in making nuclear explosives.

These developments led to immediate steps to cope with the situation. At a series of secret London meetings among the principal nuclear suppliers in 1975-77, substantial success was achieved in eliminating different treatment of non-proliferation conditions in future sales of nuclear components, related equipment and materials. (These conditions of supply are discussed later in this chapter.)

In addition to the countries[2] participating in the London meetings, Australia has recently announced that it too will adhere to the London suppliers' guidelines. These guidelines call for IAEA safeguards only in connection with the supply of a "trigger list" of specifically agreed items, rather than on all peaceful nuclear activities in recipient non-nuclear weapon countries. Non-nuclear weapon states which are parties to the NPT are already obligated by the Treaty to accept IAEA safeguards on all their peaceful nuclear facilities.

---

[2]Belgium, Canada, Czechoslovakia, France, Democratic Republic of Germany, Federal Republic of Germany, Italy, Japan, the Netherlands, Poland, Sweden, Switzerland, the United Kingdom, the United States and the Soviet Union.

TABLE I

NPT Signatories, IAEA Members, and Nuclear Suppliers (in italics)

Countries	NPT status*	IAEA member**
Afghanistan	R	yes
Albania	—	yes
Algeria	—	yes
Argentina	—	yes
Australia	R	yes
Austria	R	yes
Bahamas, The	A	no
Bangladesh	—	yes
Barbados	S	no
Belgium	R	yes
Bénin	R	no
Bolivia	R	yes
Botswana	R	no
Brazil	—	yes
Bulgaria	R	yes
Burma	—	yes
Burundi	A	no
Byelorussian SSR	(see USSR)	yes
Cameroon, United Rep. of	R	yes
Canada	R	yes
Central African Empire	A	no
Chad	R	no
Chile	—	yes
China, Republic of	R	no
Colombia	S	yes
Costa Rica	R	yes
Cuba	—	yes
Cyprus	R	yes
Czechoslovakia	R	yes

NOTES:

* As of May 1977

R=ratified   S=signed   A=deposit of accession

** As of April 1976

Denmark	R	yes
Dominican Republic	R	yes
Ecuador	R	yes
Egypt	S	yes
El Salvador	R	yes
Ethiopia	R	yes
Finland	R	yes
Fiji	A	no
France	—	yes
Gabon	A	yes
Gambia, The	R	no
German Democratic Rep.	R	yes
Germany, Federal Rep. of	R	yes
Ghana	R	yes
Greece	R	yes
Grenada	A	no
Guatemala	R	yes
Haiti	R	yes
Holy See	A	yes
Honduras	R	yes
Hungary	R	yes
Iceland	R	yes
India	—	yes
Indonesia	S	yes
Iran	R	yes
Iraq	R	yes
Ireland	R	yes
Israel	—	yes
Italy	R	yes
Ivory Coast	R	yes
Jamaica	R	yes
Japan	R	yes
Jordan	R	yes
Kampuchea	A	yes
Kenya	R	yes
Korea, Dem. People's Rep. of	—	yes
Korea, Republic of	R	yes
Kuwait	S	yes
Laos	R	no

Lebanon	R	yes
Lesotho	R	no
Liberia	R	yes
Libyan Arab Republic	R	yes
Liechtenstein	—	yes
Luxembourg	R	yes
Madagascar	R	yes
Malaysia	R	yes
Maldive Islands	R	no
Mali	R	yes
Malta	R	no
Mauritius	R	yes
Mexico	R	yes
Monaco	—	yes
Mongolia	R	yes
Morocco	R	yes
Nepal	R	no
Netherlands	R	yes
New Zealand	R	yes
Nicaragua	R	yes
Niger	—	yes
Nigeria	R	yes
Norway	R	yes
Pakistan	—	yes
Panama	R	yes
Paraguay	R	yes
Peru	R	yes
Philippines	R	yes
Poland	R	yes
Portugal	—	yes
Qatar	—	yes
Romania	R	yes
Rwanda	A	no
San Marino	R	no
Saudi Arabia	—	yes
Senegal	R	yes
Sierra Leone	A	yes
Singapore	R	yes
Somalia	R	no
South Africa	—	yes

Spain	—	yes
Sri Lanka	S	yes
Sudan	R	yes
Surinam	A	no
Swaziland	R	no
Sweden	R	yes
Switzerland	R	yes
Syrian Arab Republic	R	yes
Tanzania, United Rep. of	—	yes
Thailand	A	yes
Togo	R	no
Tonga	A	no
Trinidad and Tobago	S	no
Tunisia	R	yes
Turkey	S	yes
Uganda	—	yes
Ukrainian SSR	(see USSR)	yes
USSR	R	yes
United Arab Emirates	—	yes
UK	R	yes
USA	R	yes
Upper Volta	R	no
Uruguay	R	yes
Venezuela	R	yes
Viet Nam, Socialist Rep. of	R	no
Western Samoa	A	no
Yemen Arab Republic	S	no
Yemen (Aden)	S	no
Yugoslavia	R	yes
Zaire	R	yes
Zambia	—	yes

Some key recipient countries are not members of the NPT and, therefore, do not have IAEA safeguards on all their peaceful nuclear facilities. These non-NPT countries include Egypt, India, Israel, Spain, South Africa, Argentina and Brazil. In the case of these non-NPT nations, the IAEA safeguards required for nuclear exports by supplier nations (including France, not an NPT member) are not required for nuclear materials or facilities produced indigenously.

The 15 members of the enlarged London Group, including the US, have now specifically agreed that exports of trigger-list items would be made only under IAEA safeguards, that their use for "peaceful nuclear explosives" would be explicitly ruled out, and that physical security arrangements to guard against terrorist or other subnational diversion would be required in all export arrangements. On the critical issue of the "sensitive" steps of the fuel cycle, primarily uranium enrichment and reprocessing plants, the success was limited. Supplier nations have agreed to exercise "restraint" on such exports, and that any such exports would be subject to special new controls which call for non-proliferation undertakings and safeguards not only on the exported facility itself, but on any facility of the same type which the recipient nations might undertake to build. (The importance of this new safeguards principle is discussed later.) However, no agreement was reached on total prohibition of sensitive exports.

Among the principal achievements of the London effort was the inclusion of France in the suppliers' discussions and ensuing consensus. The remaining participants were already NPT parties. (See Table I). Thus, they were already complying with the treaty obligation to export nuclear materials and equipment to non-nuclear weapon states only under IAEA safeguards.

France, on the other hand, had made clear its intention *not* to adhere to the NPT; and, while it had stated that it would behave as if it were a Treaty party, it was never clear how this general principle would be extended to such specific matters as identification of those exported items which would necessitate IAEA safeguards. The recent acceptance by France of the common requirements, as well as the prerequisites going beyond the NPT, was therefore understandably viewed as a major development in French attitudes toward proliferation.

In October 1976, President Ford issued a lengthy statement on US non-proliferation policy, the first such Presidential statement to have been made since the Atoms for Peace Program was proposed by President Eisenhower in 1953. This statement carried US policy, until then dedicated to avoiding the further spread of reprocessing and plutonium to sensitive regions, a major step further. The Ford statement concluded that "the United States should no longer regard reprocessing of used nuclear fuel to produce plutonium . . . as a necessary and inevitable step in the nuclear fuel cycle . . . and that we should pursue reprocessing and recycling in the future only if they are found to be consistent with our international (non-proliferation) objectives."

President Ford did not replace the presumption of reprocessing and recycle with the opposite presumption that there would be no reprocessing or recycle. Rather, the policy was to hold the commercialization of reprocessing and recycle in abeyance, and to shift the burden of proof for proceeding to a demonstration that the proliferation risks could be effectively dealt with. Towards this end, Ford proposed a "reprocessing evaluation program." As well, President Ford avoided taking exception to the breeder reactor. He indicated that the US breeder reactor development program, concentrated like those of other nations on the plutonium-fueled, liquid metal-cooled breeder, would go forward, under the rationale that no decision on its commercialization was required or expected for at least ten years.

On April 7, 1977, President Carter, who had indicated during his Presidential campaign in 1976 that non-proliferation would be a high priority issue for his administration, took additional steps. His statement of that date called for "deferring indefinitely the commercial reprocessing and recycling of . . . plutonium" and for "restructuring (the US) breeder program to give greater priority to alternative designs . . . other than plutonium and to defer the date when breeder reactors would be put into commercial use."

Both the Ford and Carter statements recognized that the US decisions were explicitly applicable only to US reprocessing, recycle, and breeder programs, but both made clear their hope that other nations would follow the US lead, and called for international cooperation in the subsequent evaluation steps.

Like Ford, Carter proposed an international evaluation on the future shape of the nuclear fuel cycle, but with a significant difference. Where Ford proposed an evaluation of reprocessing with the purpose of determining whether reprocessing and plutonium utilization could proceed in a manner compatible with non-proliferation objectives, Carter initiated an international fuel cycle evaluation with the purpose of finding acceptable alternatives to the plutonium-based fuel cycles or of providing adequate safeguards for the plutonium cycle. In short, where Ford contemplated solutions which involved learning to live with plutonium, Carter seemed inclined to finding ways to live without it.

President Carter continued to emphasize the potential relationship between sensitive technologies and nuclear weapons, although his April 7, 1977, statement recognized to a limited extent the role of reprocessing and enrichment in other states which have already made a commitment to a complete nuclear fuel cycle program. As fundamental accompaniments to a deferral of reprocessing, the administration outlined plans to establish an interim spent fuel storage program (for US domestic fuel only) and to increase US enrichment capacity. Meanwhile, key countries in the non-proliferation and nuclear power debate had agreed to participate in the US proposed International Nuclear Fuel Cycle Evaluation (INFCE). This effort is intended to afford nations an opportunity to reevaluate the relative non-proliferation and economic merits of alternative fuel cycles before confirming any widespread commitment to the plutonium cycle. Although the administration has pledged that no civilian reprocessing of power reactor spent fuel will occur in the US during the evaluation, the US has agreed to the re-processing of a limited amount of spent fuel (containing uranium enriched in the US) in the Tokai Mura facility in Japan, for a period of two years in the context of a joint safeguard and proliferation-resistant technology program. (Despite US disclaimers of precedent in this agreement, it is likely to become a source of controversy in US negotiations with other countries which may wish to reprocess fuel of US origin.)

B. The Current International Controversy

While other countries are not bound to follow US non-proliferation policy, there may be current and significant opportunities to make some progress on such issues as safeguards, sensitive transfers, reprocessing, fuel assurances, and advanced/alternative reactors. The US continues to be the major supplier, even to most of the industrialized nations, of uranium enrichment services and of some reactor equipment and technology. Moreover, in many of its agreements for cooperation it retains a qualified right to approve the location and means of reprocessing of any US-supplied material. Thus, the US is capable of exercising a degree of control over reprocessing of nuclear fuel in other nations until alternative sources of enrichment become avail-able,[3] although some of its nuclear partners disagree as to whether it has a valid legal right to do so.

If new US non-proliferation policies are to elicit needed international cooperation, then other countries' support of the US policy developments will be essential. These policies must not only be sound, but acceptable to others if they are substantially to affect nuclear power development in the future.

To date, key supplier nations have shown a readiness to follow strengthened non-proliferation policies. Guidelines adopted by the original seven supplier nations which began meeting in London in mid-1975 are set out in Appendix D. Eight additional suppliers or potential suppliers have signified their acceptance of these guidelines and have become members of the group. Australia, not a member of this group, has announced its intention to follow the same guidelines. France and the Federal Republic of Germany have indicated their intention not to enter into further arrangements involv-ing the supply of reprocessing technology for the time being. To a consider-able degree, this situation outside the US mirrored that in the US itself, where there was broad agreement on the objective of non-proliferation, and where disagreement related to means and not to goals.

However, some of the supplier nations have evidenced serious reser-vations concerning the most recent US nuclear policy developments. In their view, this new policy represents more than a strengthening or tightening of previous policy, and marks a fundamental change in direction: a return, in

---

[3]P.L. Ølgaard (Denmark) comments: The day when alternative sources of enrichment become available is likely to be precipitated if purchaser countries feel that the US uses its position to attach purely political strings to US nuclear supplies.

fact if not in name, to the policy of denial which failed to prevent the emergence of additional nuclear powers in the first post-war decade. In general, their reservations can be grouped into doubts about the effectiveness of the policy and doubts about its fairness and practicality.

First, as to doubts concerning the effectiveness of the new US policy, the views of foreign critics — as well as some of the US nuclear industry — can be summarized as follows:

(1) Nuclear power and the light water reactor fuel cycle represent not an easy way, and perhaps the most difficult, time-consuming and costly way to achieve a nuclear weapon capability, given the political acceptability within any particular country of a decision to build nuclear weapons. Information about reprocessing not only is widely available, but any moderately industrialized country has the capability to build reprocessing plants. Similarly, small reactors designed to produce plutonium can be built more easily, quickly and cheaply than power reactors. Thus, as experience to date has demonstrated, countries which are willing overtly to acquire nuclear weapons are not likely to choose the power reactor route and will not be seriously impeded in achieving nuclear weapons by withholding plutonium or sensitive parts of the power reactor fuel cycle. However, it is also true that in politically unstable situations, nationally controlled reprocessing plants and plutonium stocks could be easily converted in a short time to the weapon option.

(2) A policy of denial may stimulate independent national efforts which are subject to no control; and these efforts, whether by original intent or later decision, are more likely to lead to proliferation than is a policy of cooperation under effective controls. Providing nuclear assistance to countries which are on the threshold of achieving such capabilities on their own, in exchange for non-proliferation undertakings and safeguards on all similar facilities, may represent a more effective means to avoid proliferation than denial.

(3) Existing nuclear control arrangements, including bilateral agreements and the Non-Proliferation Treaty, and their accompanying safeguards, represent an accepted deterrent against proliferation. New measures, particularly any which can be interpreted as inconsistent with the obligations of the NPT to share peaceful nuclear energy,[4] run the risk of undermining the effectiveness of the existing non-proliferation regime, without providing any assurance that more effective measures will take its place.[5]

The reservations which relate to the fairness and practicality of the new US policies can be summarized as follows:

---

[4] Article IV(2) of the NPT provides: "All the Parties to the Treaty undertake to facilitate, and have the right to participate in, the fullest possible exchange of equipment, materials, and scientific and technological information for the peaceful uses of nuclear energy."

[5] P.L. Ølgaard (Denmark) observes: In the eyes of the NPT non-nuclear weapon countries it would seem more logical to strengthen the safeguards system for those countries who are not parties to the NPT and thus have not formally committed themselves not to acquire nuclear weapons.

(1) The United States is unique among the larger industrially advanced nations of the West in its possession of energy resources. Even with respect to the nuclear option, the US has major uranium reserves which few others possess. The readiness of the US to delay or even to forego for itself reprocessing, plutonium recycle, and the breeder, however well-intentioned, in this view represents a sacrifice that other nations cannot afford to emulate. Moreover, it intensifies the competition for the limited uranium available.

(2) For most other countries, nuclear energy (and especially the breeder) is not as much a question of energy economics as it is one of eventually reducing energy dependence and balance of payments problems. For some, the breeder is perceived to be a necessary energy alternative.

(3) Recent US estimates of uranium availability are regarded as overly optimistic.

(4) For other nations and on the basis of present knowledge, the breeder means the liquid metal-cooled breeder operating on the plutonium cycle. While there is a willingness to consider alternatives, there is no confidence that any alternative put forward so far either significantly reduces the risks of proliferation, or can be ready for deployment by the time it may be needed. The long lead times required to develop new nuclear technologies means, in the view widely held abroad, that there is no time to lose in completing development of the plutonium breeder if it is to be ready for application early in the next century.

(5) There is a growing acceptance abroad of the US view that reprocessing and plutonium recycle for light water reactors is of only marginal economic attractiveness (although its energy conservation aspects are not taken lightly). However, reprocessing is viewed as a key step in the development of breeder technology.

(6) Reprocessing is also viewed in some countries as essential to the prudent long-term management of nuclear waste, and there is reluctance abroad to proceed with the large-scale exploitation of nuclear power until the means for permanent waste management are in hand. In some instances government regulations require reprocessing and/or firm plans for waste management as a pre-condition of installing additional nuclear power plants.

(7) The failure to reprocess and to recycle recovered plutonium will lead to the accumulation of large quantities of spent fuel in many places. This accumulation could represent both a hazard to public health and an increasing proliferation risk in its own right.

(8) Finally, it is perhaps also of some significance that breeder development seems to be one area where Europeans — rightly or wrongly — feel themselves to be clearly ahead of the US. Therefore, they not only view any US effort to downplay the significance of the breeder with suspicion but they probably tend to be relatively optimistic about the results of their own programs and the applicable economics.

C. The Nub of the Problem: Access to Nuclear Explosive Material

1. *Uranium Enrichment*

In comparison with the developments described above and related largely to reprocessing and the breeder, less attention is currently being given to the proliferation dangers of national uranium enrichment capabilities (which can provide highly enriched U^{235}, a nuclear explosive material). At the moment, conventional non-proliferation thinking considers enrichment a less immediate threat than reprocessing. However, there are signs that enrichment may be an easier route to weapons material than previously thought. An understanding of this part of the nuclear power fuel cycle is therefore necessary.

In natural uranium, the fissile isotope U^{235} occurs at a concentration of less than one percent (specifically, 0.71 percent). The two most widely used uranium-burning power reactor types use either natural uranium or uranium slightly enriched in U^{235} (to a two to four percent concentration). By contrast, uranium for nuclear weapons has to be much more highly enriched (for crude weapons to more than 20 percent, and for military weapons to more than 90 percent).

At this time, the five nuclear weapon countries (the US, the USSR, the UK, France and the People's Republic of China) are able to produce significant amounts of highly enriched uranium using the gaseous diffusion process, as will the French-led consortium Eurodif[6] beginning in 1978. Urenco, a partnership of British, West German and Dutch owners, currently uses the centrifuge method to produce low-enriched uranium. South Africa has a smaller capacity of producing enriched uranium, and is talking about expanding that capacity; Brazil expects to acquire the capacity in the future; Japan has a pilot plant with plans for commercial production; and Australia is contemplating the possibility. At present, the US remains the principal free world producer, by the gaseous diffusion process, and exporter of low-enriched uranium for power reactors. Highly enriched uranium is also produced and exported by the US, for research reactors and scientific uses, and now under increasingly rigourous justification.

Whereas the gaseous diffusion process of enrichment can be used to enrich uranium to any desired level, this process, when designed to operate on a commercial scale, requires very large, capital-intensive plant and equipment, and large amounts of electricity. New enrichment technologies, such as the centrifuge process and laser isotopic separation are expected to be more efficient, less expensive, and economic in smaller plant sizes. Like gaseous diffusion, both laser and centrifuge technologies may be used, or adapted, to produce highly enriched uranium, but on a smaller scale. There is therefore a range of enrichment technologies having a broad spectrum of technical difficulty, cost, efficiency, and clandestine potential.

Today, no commercial power reactor uses highly enriched uranium as

---

[6]In addition to France, Eurodif includes Italy, Spain, Belgium and (indirectly) Iran.

fuel. Such fuel is used in the high temperature gas-cooled reactor (HTGR) developed by the General Atomic Corporation, but only one relatively small (330 MWe) demonstration unit has been operating in the US, and no new ones are planned at this time. Research on this type of reactor is being undertaken in Germany and Japan, but it seems unlikely that power reactors using highly enriched uranium will come into widespread use in the near future.

Thus, for the present at least, legitimate fuel requirements and fuel products will not lead to accumulations of weapon-grade enriched uranium. However, it will be necessary to devise safeguards procedures which will detect the production of highly enriched uranium (usable in weapons) by plants declared to be producing only low-enriched uranium as fuel for power reactors. It should also be borne in mind that if reactors which use highly enriched uranium were to prove competitive and appear worldwide, they will pose a proliferation problem some time in the future.[7]

2. *Reprocessing and Plutonium Separation*

It has long been the assumption of participants in the US nuclear power program that the reprocessing of spent fuel produced by the current light-water nuclear power reactors, and the separation and recycling of the plutonium contained in such fuel, would provide an economic supplement to low-enriched uranium and could be recycled in these reactors in the form of a mixed oxide fuel (MOX). The issue of licensing such domestic activities on a commercial basis has been before the US Nuclear Regulatory Commission (NRC), but upon the President's request, is now scheduled to be terminated.

Reprocessing facilities can provide direct access to nuclear explosive material in the form of separated plutonium. For that reason, the US has refused to export reprocessing plants, and has urged other suppliers to follow its lead. The basis for this position has been the belief that such facilities pose unique problems in terms of maintaining effective international safeguards that can help to deter diversion of plutonium for nuclear explosives. Even if safeguards in reprocessing plants could promptly detect a diversion of material, the time available in which to take effective action to prevent its use in the manufacture of nuclear explosives would be extremely short if it is assumed that the diverting nation has previously prepared a crude nuclear explosive device.

Presently,[8] France, Japan, the UK, and Eurochemic[9] have reprocessing capability of significant scale; Argentina, West Germany, India, Italy and

---

[7] It is possible to design (or re-design) such reactors to use uranium enriched to 20 percent U^{235}. It would be very difficult to use such material in nuclear explosives. However, the introduction of 20 percent enrichment would provide a high-quality feed material for covert further enrichment.

[8] Data obtained from: US Congress, House Committee on International Relations and Senate Committee on Government Affairs, *Nuclear Proliferation Fact Book,* Joint Committee Print, 95th Congress, 1st Session, 1977, Washington, D.C., US Government Printing Office, 1977, pages 197-207 inclusive.

[9] Eurochemic: an international consortium of France, Belgium, Italy, West Germany, Denmark, Spain, Austria, Norway, Portugal, Switzerland, Turkey and Sweden.

Spain have small-scale reprocessing capacity and plans for building commercial-size plants; Canada, Czechoslovakia, Norway, the Republic of
China and Yugoslavia have operated or are operating pilot or laboratory-
scale reprocessing facilities,[10] but have not announced plans to build and
operate commercial-size plants (and in the case of the Republic of China, the
lab-scale facility has been dismantled). Brazil and Pakistan, which have
never had reprocessing capacity, have announced plans to acquire the capability on a commercial scale; and Sweden has said it is considering this
option. The US, the USSR, and the People's Republic of China, the UK
and France have been operating reprocessing plants for military purposes.
Finally, in addition to these twenty five nations, several more countries must
be presumed to have some manner of reprocessing capability.

D. Implications of the Carter Initiative

The Carter administration's decision to defer domestic reprocessing is a
dramatic step in the evolution of US non-proliferation strategy. The principal reasons initially given in support of this decision include the escalating
costs of large-scale reprocessing, and the unresolved environmental,
safeguard, and security considerations, together with the expectation that
there will be enough new uranium found in time to alter significantly the US
energy resource base. These factors combined could make reprocessing and
plutonium recycle a questionable economic and commercial venture.

The major importance of the decision emerges on closer examination. For
the first time in recent years, significant international implications of US
domestic nuclear decisions were recognized and articulated by the President. Second, by action rather than rhetoric, the US has renewed its affirma-
tion, doubted by some during recent years, that commercial considerations
would be subordinated to containing the spread of nuclear weapons.

In the case of commercial reprocessing, the most important aspect of the
Carter position is its conclusion that even if the proponents of reprocessing
and recycling should prove correct on commercial grounds, the non-
proliferation concerns associated with the use of plutonium must be addressed, at least in the US domestic power program and US export policy. If
necessary, according to this thinking, the US must be prepared to sacrifice
the benefits of a supplementary source of nuclear fuel at a time of rising
uranium and enrichment costs, and to extend the time for the commercial
development of breeder reactors if this will buy time to prevent the
worldwide spread of plutonium separation capabilities.[11]

---

[10]P. L. Ølgaard (Denmark) observes: To the best of my knowledge, this should read: "Presently France and the UK have reprocessing capabilities of significant scale; Eurochemic, Japan, West Germany, India and Italy have small-scale reprocessing capacity and/or plans for
building commercial-size plants; Argentina, Canada, the Republic of China, Czechoslovakia,
Norway, Spain and Yugoslavia have . . . " i.e., according to my sources the information of
"Nuclear Proliferation Fact Book" is not correct. [See footnote[8].]

[11]David Hafemeister (United States) comments: For a slippage of $100/kWe in the capital cost
of the breeder (from the economic break-even point), it allows one to go to higher uranium
prices of $40/pound above the equilibrium uranium price. This assumes a capital multiplier of
0.16.

Worldwide expansion of uranium exploration and extraction is essential to this policy, as is the enlargement of enrichment capabilities, and the provision of adequate spent fuel storage facilities. The hope for a commitment among Canada, Australia, and the US to assure an adequate supply of uranium to cooperative states would probably have to be a fundamental ingredient of this policy. Concerning US supply of enrichment services, plans have been announced by the US to increase the capacity of diffusion plants and to build a new facility using centrifuge enrichment. The initial phase of the administration's spent fuel policy is to transfer the spent fuel to the government, which will store it first at interim sites, then at a permanent repository. There will be a one-time storage fee to the user. If the government finds reprocessing acceptable in the future, the spent fuel can then be returned with a storage charge refund, or other compensation can be provided to the user for the net fuel value. This program will be open to other countries on a limited basis, but qualifications, terms, and conditions have not yet been set. Interim sites have not yet been selected nor storage fees and refunds established.

The Carter administration policy, while broadly stated, still leaves to be implemented a number of major requirements essential to its success: measures must be developed to assure an adequate supply of low-enriched, uranium fuel for cooperating nuclear nations that use light water reactors, including steps to re-establish and strengthen the commercial role of the US as a reliable long-term supplier of such fuel; the possible establishment of an international regime for fuel services and the effective management of plutonium must be examined; increased capacity for short and long-term disposal of spent fuel must be created; and the strengthening of US export control policies to implement the new position must be assured. Redefining export policy specifically raises the issue of preferences to be given to NPT states, to those with equivalent full-scope safeguards, and to those agreeing to postpone reprocessing. As well there is the issue of the limitations on exports to other nations which refuse to be party to such measures. The Non-Proliferation Act of 1978 mandates the US to renegotiate all current nuclear agreements for cooperation among the countries concerned to incorporate the new criteria while preserving the integrity of existing governmental commitments.

The new US position has also affected US development of the liquid metal fast breeder reactor (LMFBR). While President Carter wants to terminate the Clinch River LMFBR project, Western Europe and Japan have remained committed to early commercialization of breeders, and the Soviet Union has given its breeder program a high national energy priority.

It seems unlikely that there will be early acceptance among the developed countries of the proposition to rely solely on current reactors. Moreover, as long as the developing countries observe continued reprocessing taking place in the developed countries, they are unlikely to be fully convinced that reprocessing is not a necessary part of a viable nuclear program as it applies to their own needs. They may simply write off the significance of the US position as *sui generis* — one simply reflecting the unique position of the US as the possessor of large uranium (and coal) reserves and immense uranium enrichment capacity. They may also continue to suspect and assert that a hidden motive for the US position is to pursue the commercial objective of extending the US's profitable role as the dominant supplier of enrichment services and a major supplier of light water reactors.[12]

With some prospect of greater nuclear independence in the long term by the use of breeders, the developing countries may not likely be content. There is sensitivity among LDCs about the asymmetries of the NPT, and about the London Nuclear Suppliers' Group.

Deferral of reprocessing in the US, even when coupled with rigorous export controls at home and supplier guidelines abroad, is not a sufficient answer to controlling the spread of plutonium around the world. The withholding of technology from developing countries could well aggravate rather than reduce the problem of controlling the spread of nuclear weapons capabilities.

The answer, in the opinion of many, does not lie solely in asking how a country might use nuclear power to make nuclear weapons, and making it more difficult to do so. Such attempts may fail if a country is determined to build nuclear weapons. The answer is seen to lie therefore at least in part in addressing those underlying security and political concerns of the individual threshold countries which result in their perceiving their "supreme national interest" to be enhanced by the acquisition of nuclear weapons in the first place.

E. Developing Countries and Nuclear Proliferation

The central principle of the NPT and the IAEA has been the concept of international cooperation in peaceful nuclear development, mainly for electric power supply, in return for a forswearing by non-weapon states of weapons acquisition, and acceptance by them of international safeguards. It is doubtful that the alternative of denial and sanctions could ever have succeeded, but under today's conditions and prospects the development and diffusion of technology and relevant skills make that alternative clearly unworkable and incapable of achieving its ostensible non-proliferation objective.

This concept inherently entails discrimination between nuclear weapon states and non-weapon states. To be acceptable, a non-proliferation policy based on international cooperation for peaceful development should come as close as possible to symmetry and non-discrimination in nuclear energy development. Only in this way can institutional arrangements for nuclear fuel

---

[12]Richard L. Garwin (United States) comments: As I have mentioned in the Working Group discussions, one could eliminate suspicions as to the "profit" by having the US supply enrichment at zero cost with new technologies as they come along.

P. L. Ølgaard (Denmark) comments: They may also fear that the US might use its position as a major nuclear supplier for pure political purposes, making the developing countries more dependent on the US.

cycle options which offer increased proliferation resistance effectively take account of the interests and sensitivities of the less-developed countries.

In particular, while technical assistance should be freely available to assist developing countries in assessing their energy needs and alternative supply possibilities, there should be no *a priori* judgment that a permanent class of "third world" countries has no need for nuclear energy. The aim would be identical treatment for all non-weapon states willing to forswear explosive devices and accept international full-scope safeguards. It should be recognized that the most likely candidates for proliferation are precisely those developing countries that are already substantially industrialized and should be moving out of the category of "third world" or "developing" nations during the next decade or two. Development of a cooperative approach to non-proliferation requires the participation of all states with a serious interest in nuclear energy development, rather than confrontation between a supplier group and recipients.

F. Two Kinds of Proliferation

While an approach focusing on the individual situation of each of some 10 or 20 current weapon threshold countries can prove successful, it can do so only in the short term, for additional countries are bound to arrive at that same threshold in the course of their economic and technological development. In other words, there must be a distinction made between two kinds of proliferation that concern today's policy makers. The first kind is a country-specific scenario of nations close to weapon capability now: the near-term proliferation problem. It is this problem that must be dealt with on a case-by-case basis. The second kind of proliferation, the longer-term problem, relates to the worldwide advancement in nuclear and other industrial technologies: a more general and abstract problem, but nonetheless real.

The country-specific, near-term proliferation problem can be addressed through export policies, sanctions, supply security and regional security guarantees and other measures that involve incentives and disincentives tailored to individual nations' perceived needs. The more general, longer-term proliferation threat is clearly what the Carter administration policy makers have in mind in reevaluating alternative fuel cycles, attempting to control the role of plutonium in future nuclear power. The most difficult aspect of this approach is that it is discriminatory; the problem becomes one of defining those "qualified" (for using plutonium) without antagonizing others. The key to success may be for policy makers to keep firmly in mind that the primary purpose of the international system they are forming is to meet energy requirements as well as non-proliferation goals.

G. Alternative Routes to Nuclear Weapons

A non-NPT country which has no obligation to accept IAEA safeguards on all its facilities, but intends to develop nuclear weapons, might well decide to take a route that is more direct and less expensive (in political and financial terms) and is at the same time independent of civilian nuclear power and of facilities requiring outside assistance and safeguards. One such route, taken by the nuclear weapon states in the past, has been the construction of "plutonium production" reactors to provide the explosive material. These are essentially natural uranium "production" or even "research" reactors, versions of which already exist throughout the world using widely known technology.

Such small natural uranium reactors have a number of advantages for a country with nuclear weapons ambitions. They do not require enriched uranium, with attached safeguards, and operate at room temperature and atmospheric pressure. Natural uranium can be purchased on the world market, and the reactor can be built indigenously, unlike a large nuclear power plant that has to be purchased from suppliers and therefore safeguarded. There are fewer complications than with large power reactors in dealing with high temperatures and pressures and in the handling of highly radioactive spent fuel elements.

Because neither natural uranium nor indigenous reactors are subject to safeguards in a non-NPT state, the plutonium-bearing spent fuel would not be subject to safeguards either. It would therefore be possible for such a country to construct a small processing plant capable of separating plutonium without outside assistance and hence without safeguards. Thus, there is nothing to prevent a non-NPT country from producing a nuclear device with no violation of safeguards or other international commitment.

However, this may overstate the ease with which non-NPT countries could produce a nuclear explosive device without violating safeguards or other international commitments. There is no guarantee that such a country could purchase natural uranium on the world market without agreeing to safeguards. Moreover, it is not clear that a non-NPT country would have the necessary skills, equipment or materials to build a production reactor entirely on its own, without outside assistance or purchases. Finally, it should be pointed out that at least as far as the US is concerned the acquisition of a nuclear explosive device could result in the termination of US nuclear supplies.

In contrast to production or research reactors, clandestine diversion of material for nuclear weapons purposes from civilian nuclear power facilities is difficult, and involves a substantial risk of detection. It follows that the most promising way of controlling the spread of nuclear weapons capabilities is not to reduce nuclear exports, but to channel nuclear development through the continued transfer of safeguarded nuclear power technology, if all other nuclear activities are placed under safeguards and there are adequate sanctions. As nations come to rely more and more on power reactors to meet their growing energy needs the incentives to cheat on safeguards decrease rapidly with their increasing vulnerability to sanctions on supplies by the world nuclear community.

However, in pursuing the nuclear power route, a nation can build up a large inventory of plutonium-bearing spent fuel. If it acquires a reprocessing plant, for the avowedly peaceful purpose of plutonium recycle, it is provided with an overt way to build up a stockpile of separated plutonium. It could then be in a position close to nuclear explosive capability (by designing and prefabricating a weapon assembly in advance), an option which it could exercise if it decided to abrogate international obligations and risk counteraction. There are no safeguards on the advanced preparation of "nonnuclear" detonating mechanisms (although such activity, if detected, would probably be in violation of the NPT).

H. The Role of Plutonium

Plutonium separation has come to be regarded as a basic point of connection between nuclear power and nuclear weapon capabilities. The new US position seeks to keep these activities as separate as possible. As long as countries continue building nuclear plants fueled by natural uranium or low-enriched uranium (which are not explosive materials) and as long as the plutonium-bearing spent fuel is held indefinitely in storage, countries producing nuclear power will be kept one additional stage removed from nuclear weapon capability. Safeguards systems to detect diversion in these circumstances can operate effectively and give warning of diversion. However, once countries engage in reprocessing and plutonium recycle, for light water reactors or for fast breeder reactors, or both, the line between nuclear power and nuclear weapons is no longer the presence of separated plutonium but the use of the separated plutonium, for a fuel element in a reactor or the explosive material of a bomb.[13]

If stockpiles of plutonium accumulate in national hands, international safeguards as a means of detecting diversion, and therefore of deterring it by providing advance warning, become less meaningful. Even if safeguards work perfectly, the warning signal would come only when the plutonium is taken from the stockpile, presumably for insertion into a pre-constructed explosive device.

Recognition of this risk has led many to redefine the decisive steps of proliferation, heretofore assumed to occur when a country detonates a nuclear explosive device and thereby *demonstrates* nuclear weapon capability. The usual, limited definition of proliferation reflects the NPT commitment not to manufacture or acquire a nuclear weapon or any other nuclear explosive — a forbidden act that is demonstrated by detonation. Dr. Fred C. Iklé, former Director of the US Arms Control and Disarmament Agency (ACDA), suggested that the US may be developing a new concept of proliferation. He argued, in 1976, that the *acquisition* of a reprocessing plant by Pakistan, which had no commercial justification given its primitive nuclear program, was in itself an act of proliferation.

---

[13]David Hafemeister (United States) comments: It is useful to point out here that plutonium is less valuable (5/7 of U^{235}) in thermal reactors (Pu breeding ratio of about 1.2-1.3 vs. about 1.0 for U^{235}).

I. International Control: Two Schools of Thought

Two schools of thought are found in the current debate on international controls. The first takes the position that in producing plutonium fuels, access to weapon-usable fissile material would put a great burden — both political and technical — on the current non-proliferation regime: nations could prepare a nuclear weapon option without actually diverting weapon-usable material and assembling a weapon, thereby not quite violating their non-proliferation commitments but effectively eliminating the possibility of safeguards technically detecting the actual diversion of weapon-usable material in time to make any difference.

A second school of thought is based on the concept of proliferation which distinguishes the actual manufacture or acquisition of nuclear weapons or explosives from the development of nuclear power, even when it involves the use of separated plutonium. The core of this position is that the assured capability of the safeguards system to provide timely warning of diversion could preserve its deterrent effects if fortified by a greatly strengthened regime of sanctions and penalties for any material violation of a non-weapon commitment or of safeguards agreements. These sanctions would be extended by suppliers' agreement to embrace all nuclear facilities of all countries receiving any outside assistance or supply of fuel, facilities, or know-how. Both the terms of these sanctions and the commitment of other states to them would be made clear at the outset of continued trade. If sanctions and penalties are drastic enough to affect non-nuclear as well as nuclear programs that depend on outside assistance, and if the suppliers stick together in applying sanctions, the second school of thought contends that however close a nation comes to an immediate nuclear weapon option capability, the nation will hesitate to exercise it if the assured worldwide response is sufficiently immediate and severe.

The first school of thought would reduce the temptation of possession of legally authorized nuclear explosive materials. The second school of thought emphasizes the deterrent effect of prompt, assured and drastic action in the event of a violation. Neither school would reject the usefulness of a period of reevaluation, nor the possibility of multinational collective action to reduce non-proliferation risks. The first school rejects the early prospects of coping with separated plutonium by any means. The second school is less certain that proliferation objectives can be satisfied by withholding technologies exploiting the energy potential of plutonium.

Two major multinational approaches have been suggested as alternatives to the international sale of reprocessing plants. One approach is the establishment of multinationally owned and operated fuel cycle centers, which have been the subject of an IAEA study. The other is the provision of centralized fuel cycle services, national or multinational or both, located in international enclaves within supplier territories.

However, the US has become increasingly concerned that international fuel cycle centers might attract and accelerate interest in reprocessing, and that the creation of such centers might strengthen the economic and technological case for plutonium recycle at an earlier date. The US is therefore discussing establishing such centers in nuclear weapon states, and perhaps limiting their function initially to spent fuel storage. Consideration is being given to proposals that these centers receive spent fuel and provide in return an equivalent value of low-enriched uranium.

J. Nuclear Proliferation and Arms Control

If they are to prove to be broadly acceptable and effective, measures to control the proliferation of nuclear weapon capabilities should be balanced by obligations to control the growth and sophistication of current nuclear arsenals. President Carter early in his administration therefore called for negotiation of a multilateral, comprehensive nuclear test ban.

The goal of a comprehensive test ban is to halt completely any testing which serves to advance nuclear weapon development anywhere in the world. As President Carter stated in 1977 before the United Nations, " . . . the time has come to end all explosions of nuclear devices, no matter what their claimed justification — peaceful or military." A comprehensive test ban would impose limitations on nuclear weapon states and non-nuclear weapon states alike.

Successful negotiation of a comprehensive test ban would constitute a landmark arms control achievement — slowing the qualitative weapons competition among the nuclear weapon states. For the nuclear weapon states, it could lead to reduced dependence on nuclear weapons. For the non-nuclear weapon states, it could substantially reduce the incentives to develop a technology leading to a nuclear explosive capability. For both, it would serve as an important measure to support collective non-proliferation efforts.

The UN Conference of the Committee on Disarmament (CCD) in Geneva has become the key institution for the negotiation of multilateral arms control agreements. Three of the world's nuclear weapon states (the United Kingdom, the Soviet Union and the United States) have since the autumn of 1977 been engaged in serious negotiations directed towards achieving such a test ban.

The issues involved in these negotiations are complex and difficult. They have repeatedly thwarted earlier efforts to achieve a negotiated test ban. Nevertheless, cautiously optimistic reports have been made by the Carter Administration. Substantial progress has been reported towards agreement on the provisions of a treaty prohibiting nuclear weapon tests and a protocol covering nuclear explosions for peaceful purposes which would be an integral part of the treaty. It is hoped that the Conference of the Committee on Disarmament will be able in the near future to begin consideration of the results of these trilateral negotiations.

K. The Emerging Issue: The Future of the Breeder Reactor

Implicit in the statements of Presidents Ford and Carter is the thought that a choice does not have to be made now between nuclear power, as currently produced by light water reactors, and non-proliferation. Explicit in President Carter's statement is the further recognition that a decision ultimately will be needed on plutonium-fueled nuclear power, although the deadline for this decision has not been set.

The repercussions of the new position, which emphasizes the proliferation dangers of the plutonium breeder cycle, are already widespread. President Carter speaks of a deferral of commercialization of breeders while accepting the need for this long-term option, and the fact that breeders and reprocessing are inextricably related. Realistically, it must be noted that any nation which has successfully developed the breeder and considers it as a necessary or prudent addition to its resource base is probably going to deploy it, in the absence of some compelling restraint, as soon as its development has established its economic and political practicability. The breeder reactor debate and the specific issues behind it are examined in detail in the following chapter.

II. THE NEW BREEDER REACTOR DEBATE [1]

A. Introduction

In dealing with the future of breeder reactors and their potential effect upon nuclear proliferation, it is essential to have a perspective of the principal issues which drive the current debate. The purpose of this chapter is to focus on these issues.

The main issues dominating the debate are:

- *Resource Depletion.* The breeder can be perceived as a means of forestalling (or as insurance against) a global and extended energy crisis.
- *Assurance of Supply.* The breeder can be perceived as a means of reducing dependence on uncertain foreign energy supplies.
- *Health, Safety & Environment.* The breeder can be perceived as an unnecessary source of health, safety and environmental risks and costs.
- *Energy Economics.* The breeder can be viewed as a means of slowing spiraling energy costs.
- *Public Acceptance.* The breeder can be viewed either as consistent with the desires of the majority of the public, or as the choice of special interest groups.
- *Non-proliferation.* The breeder can be perceived as an unnecessary contributor to the nuclear weapons proliferation problem.

B. The Resource Depletion Issue

The case for the breeder suggests that uncertainties regarding resource sufficiency require the development of an effective "insurance policy" technology capable of deployment if optimistic resource scenarios do not materialize, and that the best (for some industrial nations, the only) such technology is the breeder. Although almost any nation can argue effectively for immediate *development* of breeder reactors, it is more difficult to make a compelling case for extensive commercial *deployment* at this time even if proven commercial technology existed.

The resource argument, which compels *development,* is based on indications of the extent of the resource base. Although expert opinion displays a wide range for the expected timing of global resource depletion, a significant body of opinion holds that uranium shortages could occur as early as in the next 25 years and almost certainly within the next 50. Compared to conse-

[1]This chapter on the driving issues behind the breeder reactor debate has been developed with the help of an ongoing review and assessment of national policies and international cooperation on breeders, undertaken under other auspices by the Chairman and several members of the Working Group and others, at the behest and with the support of the Rockefeller Foundation. We are most grateful for the early access provided to that work.

quences which would accompany such near-term depletion, the costs of breeder development are small.[2] Many countries therefore feel prudent planning suggests that, by the end of the century, a technology be tested, proven and available, and that this technology be capable of sustaining their national energy economies.

The timing needs of each nation vary, but the long lead times inherent in the research, development and demonstration (RD&D) process suggest that any technology selected for deployment should be under development now. From a practical standpoint, dependence on technologies which have not already achieved some of the more advanced research, development and demonstration milestones may be a dangerous gamble.

For much of the world, the liquid metal breeder reactor is the technology of choice for development. Advanced converters and other breeders are generally viewed as having at least the same overall lead times and development costs (actually, considerably more, since serious RD&D has not yet started) and at best marginal improvement in proliferation aspects. The positions are currently being reevaluated in the course of the International Nuclear Fuel Cycle Evaluation (INFCE).

Deployment of breeders to forestall resource depletion is a complicated proposition which would be difficult to plan centrally on an international basis, particularly as commercial breeders have not yet been developed. In most nations, the deployment decision is affected by a vast number of interrelated and changing interest groups. In each national decisions system, these groups include: the R&D establishment, usually the government; the "vendors" and constructors of the nuclear plants and services, whether or not they are "private" firms; the users of the technology, i.e., the electric utilities, regardless of the nature of their ownership; and the "public" together with its representatives and spokesmen. Further complicating the issue, these sectors are themselves by no means monolithic. If a consensus could be developed among these interest groups, a workable long-range deployment plan might be achievable. In practice, consensus of this sort is rare.

It is therefore difficult for most nations explicitly to consider the deployment decision in a centralized way. Instead, it may be necessary for them to postpone the deployment decision until the technology, resource base and price issues have been resolved, and health, safety, environmental and safeguards requirements are met. At a minimum this means until the technology is "proven" on the scale of commercial size reactors. Before such proof of commercial viability, deployment is a high risk venture. However, in some nations (e.g., France) the government and industrial sectors hold the view that the time when such proof is available is very near. Nevertheless it is possible, in most nations and to a large degree, to decouple the development and deployment activities, and consequently, the respec-

---

[2]However, paying the cost of breeder development does nothing more than provide an option which must then be successfully demonstrated and deployed to have any effect.

tive decisions. It should be noted that under this approach, if the breeder were developed and later not deployed, the investment would be lost: such is the nature of an "insurance policy". However, an eventual decision not to deploy would not imply that the development decision had been incorrect. In approaching the problem this way, decision makers in each country and in each sector would agree explicitly to recognize that the resource issue is characterized by uncertainty, and is likely to remain so for many years. The debate would benefit from such recognition.

C. The Assurance of Supply Issue

Nations are likely to make development/deployment decisions on the breeder in light of their individual energy supply/demand situation, with consideration of global resources as secondary. On this basis, industrialized nations which lack large domestic reserves of mineral energy resources generally view it as necessary to develop breeders as soon as possible and to deploy them on a timely basis. The global resource problem is therefore somewhat less relevant than it would appear at first.

Discussion with individual national representatives and review of published policy statements confirms that each nation tends to view the elements of the resource issue from the point of view of its own needs, reserves, and a usually negative perception of access to reserves owned by others. There is every indication that this attitude will persist in the future, particularly since extensive public concern over, and scrutiny of assurance of, uranium supply has made it more difficult for governments to be flexible in this regard. Even if politically motivated cooperative arrangements on resources were adopted to an unusual extent, balance-of-payment problems would continue to stimulate the desire for increased self-sufficiency.

Since each nation faces different indigenous reserves and different demand growth prospects, each will face its resource crisis at different times. For example, the West Germans perceive themselves as dangerously close to the end of their domestic energy resource base; the US on the other hand has domestic energy options. Each nation views itself and others as being at particular points on the resource criticality spectrum. The varying levels of need and technological and economic ability make a concerted worldwide transition to low or cooperative resource consumption strategies extremely difficult to achieve and most unlikely.

However, in general, within the national decision-making structures — other than in the US — the potential dangers of a plutonium economy tend to be viewed as less troublesome than the dangers of interruptible and/or high-cost foreign energy supply. Several industrial nations are therefore likely to continue to pursue breeders as part of their national energy policies. In particular, this applies to France, the Federal Republic of Germany, the UK, Japan and the USSR. US policy remains in flux, and is currently organized to continue breeder R&D while deferring actual demonstration of the reactor.

D. The Health, Safety and Environmental Issues

Satisfactory resolution of the health, safety and environmental issues is essential for breeders to achieve the acceptability (political, technological, and popular) needed for widespread deployment. The situation for LMFBRs may benefit from the extended debate which has accompanied the maturing of the conventional nuclear reactor industry.

The comparison of the evolution of conventional health, safety and environmental issues, and the process of resolving those issues for breeders yield several helpful insights. First, "resolution" of the issues never fully occurs. Instead, the systems gradually become safer and more expensive while public acceptance of the technology increases. Eventually, public spokesmen deem the technology more-or-less "safe", and new health, safety and environmental improvements as well as related cost increases occur more marginally. The public has in effect at that point decided that it has purchased all the safety it can (or will) pay for.

Second, if the system does not reach public acceptability before its costs escalate beyond economic acceptability, it will likely not be deployed. There is evidence that conventional (light water reactor) nuclear technology has reached the point of health, safety and environmental acceptability. Some of this evidence is to be found in several endorsements by independent public and quasi-public evaluatory groups.[3] There are some indications that this evolutionary process for health, safety and environmental acceptance of nuclear technology is more advanced in the US and Japan than in Europe. But it is impossible to say that this is so with confidence. Just as breeders are in an early stage of technological development, relative to conventional nuclear technology, they are as well in the early stages of defining health, safety and environmental acceptability. For breeders, public evaluation of these aspects should be less tortuous, due to knowledge on the part of the industry, policy makers, regulatory bodies and the public, of the process.

Specifically, there appear to be three fundamental areas of health, safety and environmental concern: loss of coolant/coolant flow (and related core-melt problems); toxicity of plutonium; and waste disposal. For each of these areas of concern, technical solutions are currently under investigation. Part of the engineering process for resolving these outstanding issues is the construction and operation of demonstration projects; and it is likely that satisfactory resolution of these issues will not be reached until such demonstration. International cooperation on health, safety and the environment has the potential to improve the institutional approval process and the technical solutions as well.

---

[3]Royal Commission on Environmental Pollution, Sir Brian Flowers, Chairman, in the UK.

Ranger Uranium Environmental Enquiry, Justice R. W. Fox, Presiding Commissioner, in Australia.

Nuclear Energy Policy Study Group, Spurgeon M. Keeny, Chairman, sponsored by the Ford Foundation, administered by the Mitre Corporation, in the US.

E. Economic Issues

Two important characteristics of breeder economics may be noted: first, economics will be a major force in determining when and if breeders can be successfully deployed; and second, the economics of both the capital plant and the fuel cycle over the next 20 to 30 years are so uncertain as to be considered speculative.

With regard to the first point, it should be emphasized that other factors such as assurance of supply, utility confidence, and public acceptance are also important. However, while other factors can create some deployment despite unfavorable economics, there is historical evidence to support the proposition that deployment would not be continued indefinitely unless the resulting electric generation costs are favorable (compared to all viable options). This is likely to be especially true under possible future conditions of capital scarcity.

With regard to the second point, although many economic uncertainties exist, some generalities regarding the nature of the economics are identifiable. First, the breeder's entire claim to advantage relative to conventional reactors lies in its potentially cheaper fuel cycle, virtually decoupling fuel price from the natural constraints of uranium scarcity, uneven world distribution, and exploration uncertainties. The LMFBR fuel cycle is more capital- and technology-intensive than thermal reactor cycles (once-through fuel cycle or recycle).

Power plant capital costs are projected as being considerably higher than those of light water reactors. The authors of the cost projections, without the actual experience of having built and operated plants of commercial size, have room for wide variations. Even modern light water reactors in the United States vary widely in cost depending on where they are built and by whom.

The extent and nature of these economic uncertainties lead to the conclusion that breeders will only be economical if fuel prices continue to rise, to the point where fuel cycle cost savings outweigh increased capital plant costs. This seems likely to happen, if one believes even the mild resource scarcity scenarios. How much fuel prices must rise to make the breeder competitive is indeed speculative, since without commercially sized reactor experience, breeder capital costs are themselves speculative. However, sufficient data exist to indicate that there is high likelihood that breeder costs will be competitive with conventional sources of electric power at some point around the turn of this century.

It may therefore be concluded that the only way to reduce the economic uncertainties is to build at least a few commercial-scale demonstration breeders. This may turn out to be an expensive proposition, especially if the economics do not prove out and the breeder is therefore (or for some other reason) not deployed. However, the potential economic pay-off over the years ahead, if the breeder can be made to be an economic success, is so large as to dwarf the cost of development.

F. The Impact of Public Acceptance on Breeder Cooperation

One of the main differences among national systems is the importance of public acceptance. While public acceptance is clearly not a concern of the Soviet breeder program, in the West it is an important facet of the issue. However, it is virtually impossible to judge its strength, direction and degree of importance in each system.

At a minimum, it can be said that in the US, the UK, West Germany, France and Japan, pursuit of breeder reactor programs, especially where these entail international cooperation, requires public acceptance and support. Each system has its own means of translating public opinion into public policy.

G. The Non-Proliferation Issue

While there is worldwide concern over the non-proliferation issue, and a new readiness to seek more effective measures to contain proliferation, deferral of the breeder should not be viewed as simplifying the proliferation problems. On the contrary, efforts by one nation to seriously inhibit breeder development in another are likely to be viewed as intrusive and possibly threatening. Institutional arrangements which limit the number and geographic spread of facilities and which place those which do emerge under some improved form of international control may represent a more promising approach to controlling potential proliferation risk engendered by breeder deployment. By increasing friction and thereby reducing chances for an international accord on plutonium control, attempts to solve the proliferation issue by unilateral national controls or conditions on the export of fuel cycle materials and services may further weaken assurances of supply, and lead to more rapid and less considered deployment of breeders.

This viewpoint follows from an assessment of several technological and political factors. First, plutonium is already available from other sources. In particular, reprocessing technology is widely available and within the capabilities of many moderately industrialized nations. Even if the light water reactor economy is operated on a once-through basis, there will be large amounts of plutonium in reactor cores and spent fuel inventories which can be diverted or seized and reprocessed by nations to yield separated plutonium.

It can be argued that increased availability of and trading in plutonium may make it difficult to assess whether a non-weapon nation is using it for reactor or weapon purposes. This problem may or may not actually materialize depending on the type of controls involved. Further, most nations which have any reasonable need for breeders in the near future either already are weapon states, or already are capable of becoming weapon states if they were to choose to do so.

One essential conclusion is that the ability of the world community to limit nuclear weapons proliferation depends primarily on the existence of an internationally shared political will to do so. Technology *per se* can neither cause proliferation nor prevent it, if sustained motivation and commitment are lacking. Efforts to limit proliferation must be carefully focused on influencing that motivation and commitment toward restriction of weapons.

Second, the risk of diversion of weapon-grade material by terrorists should be recognized as a problem distinct from the national proliferation issue. It is in the interest of all nations to reach a solution to this problem and as a result the issue is more manageable. Currently, a number of possible concepts are available to address the problem which, when combined, could provide adequate protection. These include effective material accounting, and appropriate location of facilities. Given the availability of these defenses, there is little reason to forego an important energy option (such as the breeder) solely to avoid the risk of terrorist action — a risk which can be, and has been, controlled through safeguards against theft and sabotage.

Third, several nations view the potential problems associated with a plutonium economy as subordinate to the problem of the assurance of supply, and are therefore intent on pursuing breeders in some form. If any nation succeeds in deploying LMFBRs, there is less incentive for other nations to forego them on non-proliferation grounds.

It is also worthwhile to note that the same perceived resource and economic pressures which lead Western Europe and Japan to favor breeders in general, lead to reluctance on their part to consider alternative fuel cycles as a non-proliferation remedy. The cost of abandoning the presently most advanced technology (LMFBR) in favor of a less developed reactor system may be high. The cost would be highest in Western Europe and the US, where most of the work on the LMFBR has been done.

While alternative fuel cycles should be carefully explored, current thinking seems to indicate that proliferation resistance may derive more from careful control of the fuel cycle and restrictions on exports than from choosing an alternative reactor system. If these indications are supported by the results of the INFCE, it may stimulate further support from the European Community (including France and West Germany) and Japan for institutionalizing fuel cycle controls and, possibly, export policy. But it is unlikely to stimulate support for abandoning the LMFBR plutonium system.

While there are now firm pro-breeder positions on the part of the European Community and Japan, there is also apparent agreement on the importance of the non-proliferation issue and a desire to work cooperatively toward acceptable institutional solutions. These could include: restrictions on fuel cycle activity, if organized explicitly not to interfere with (or better, to support) assurance of supply; technological modifications which do not involve major departures from the most developed technology (e.g., pre-irradiation of mixed oxide fuels); export restrictions on the breeder and related fuel cycle technologies.

However, realism requires recognition that these are not easy solutions either. Arrangements which involve restrictions on where and how sensitive fuel cycle activities can be performed may meet with resistance since they can run counter to strong feelings for energy independence, and aggravate

balance-of-payments problems. Agreement on international institutional arrangements of this type may be difficult. Export restriction may be an
interim solution but does not solve the problem of (and may even stimulate)
eventual independent development of the technology in non-supplier nations. Nevertheless, it would appear that most if not all nations are now
highly sensitive to and concerned about proliferation, and may well be willing to forego some "reasonable" degree of autonomy in their nuclear fuel
supply programs in return for an increased level of assurance on the proliferation concerns. The evolution of these concerns, their historical foundations
and their current reflection in national policy, are described in the following
chapter — as a necessary precursor to consideration of alternative policy options for the future.

III. HOW WE GOT WHERE WE ARE

A. Early Background

Few topics have been the subject of more intensive debate and study in the recent past than of the relationship between nuclear proliferation — the spread of atomic weapons to additional countries — and nuclear power. While other considerations, such as environmental and safety aspects, must be taken into account in assessing the role of nuclear power in meeting future energy needs, the potential risk of proliferation in the final analysis is the issue which sets nuclear power apart from other energy technologies. It is this issue which requires that decisions for both national programs and international cooperation be reached in a manner which transcends conventional economic and commercial considerations.

Review of the literature indicates that some misunderstanding of the background of US policy still persists, and influences current thinking on proliferation. More importantly, the conclusions which are frequently drawn, even from agreed premises, reveal a divergence in value judgments which seems surprisingly large in light of the general availability of an agreement on the relevant factual background.

The concern that the widespread application of nuclear power may contribute to the spread of nuclear weapons arises from a simple and unfortunate fact: every form of nuclear fission power conceived of to date involves either the use, or the generation, or both, of materials which are capable of being fashioned into nuclear explosives, or which, at the very minimum, represent significant steps along the paths by which weapon-usable materials can be obtained. Reactors fueled by natural or slightly enriched uranium, accounting for virtually all of the power reactors in use today, produce plutonium as an inevitable byproduct. Reactors can be devised which would be fueled with highly concentrated fissionable material — U^{235} itself, plutonium or U^{233}—and which would contain little or no fertile material for conversion to new fissionable material. However, such reactors would not only be uneconomic energy producers, but their initial fuel material would itself be capable of sustaining a nuclear explosion — hardly a convincing solution to the proliferation problem.

The view that nuclear power carries with it a significantly increased risk of nuclear proliferation rests on more than the physical fact that nuclear power reactors produce, or are fueled with, weapon-usable fissionable material. However, the belief that the production of weapon-usable fissionable material, not the development and fabrication of nuclear weapons themselves, is the principal technical barrier to proliferation rests on several facts and judgments of long standing. In the wartime development of the atomic bomb by the United States, the vast majority of the effort and resources devoted to the creation of the first nuclear explosives, estimated to cost some two billion dollars at then current prices, was devoted to the development, construction, and operation of the facilities for the production of uranium-235 and plutonium, both of which were used in the earliest nuclear weapons.

In contrast, the effort devoted to the development, design, and testing of the bomb itself was, in material and financial terms, relatively small, even by the standards of those days. This statement, however, obscures the intellectual difficulty of the task of initial bomb design. Illustrious scientific talent was gathered in the Los Alamos effort. The path to the development of the plutonium bomb, in particular, was filled with technical obstacles of the greatest difficulty, with an outcome that was by no means always certain. In contrast, the development of the U^{235} bomb, while still a major scientific achievement, was more straightforward and of far higher certainty of success. The design of the U^{235} weapon that was exploded over Hiroshima had never been tested.

It is, perhaps, a tribute to the creators of the first atomic bombs, who, as the senior scientists of the day, played an especially influential role in reaching the early judgments on the containment of weapons proliferation, that they viewed the production of fissionable materials, and not the design of bombs, as the crucial obstacle to the spread of atomic weapons. They were convinced that the scientific task which they had executed could be reproduced elsewhere by others, and that the basic scientific principles would inevitably become widely known and understood.

The result of this early analysis of the proliferation issue was incorporated into the Acheson-Lilienthal plan, which, with some modifications, became the proposal for nuclear control presented to the United Nations by Bernard Baruch in June of 1946. It stressed the importance of controlling the sensitive steps in the production of fissionable materials, and proposed the creation of an International Atomic Development Authority which would be given a worldwide monopoly for the performance of critical operations and the ownership, possession, and use of strategic nuclear materials. Thus, no individual nation would have been authorized to have direct physical access to the materials which could be fashioned into nuclear weapons. Security was to be further assured by geographic distribution of sensitive facilities and materials and by avoiding unduly large concentrations of sensitive materials in any individual country. If seizure were to occur, a possibility which was not overlooked, then at least other nations in whose territory sensitive facilities were located would not be at a disadvantage.

The emphasis on control of production facilities and materials did not, of course, mean that weapons themselves were ignored or that weapon information was allowed to pass into the public domain. The plan itself proposed the eventual abolition of nuclear weapons, and the US regarded information on weapon design as the most sensitive and highly classified of all the body of nuclear information.

The proposal clearly recognized the high likelihood that many nations would acquire the capability for fissionable materials production, as well as bomb design and manufacture. Contrary to some current perceptions of the proposal, its emphasis on international ownership and operation was based not so much on keeping production facilities out of the hands of individual nations, but on a belief that only an international organization that was directly involved in the affirmative tasks of development, design and operation of nuclear facilities could acquire the competence to inspect for unauthorized facilities of this type. The authors were also concerned that the degree of inspection necessary to ensure that nationally operated facilities were not contributing to military programs would be unacceptable.

The Baruch plan was rejected by the Soviet Union, and the special United Nations commission was allowed to expire. Concurrently, the US Congress placed the nation's nuclear effort — both military and civilian — under a five-man civilian Atomic Energy Commission, and prescribed strict limitations on the dissemination of nuclear information, both domestically and abroad, with heavy penalties for violations.

The first Soviet atomic device was exploded in 1949, considerably earlier than many had anticipated. The first British nuclear explosion occurred in 1952. While no additional countries exploded a nuclear device until 1960, when the first French explosion occurred, the handwriting was on the wall much earlier. By 1953, nuclear reactors were in operation in France, Canada, and Norway, in addition to the US, the UK, and the Soviet Union. Atomic energy programs were being initiated in numerous countries. The limited confidence that proliferation could be deferred by the policy of secrecy prescribed by the McMahan Act was eroding.

B. The Eisenhower Proposal and Atoms-for-Peace

It was against this background that President Eisenhower proposed before the United Nations General Assembly on December 7, 1953, a dramatic reversal in US and worldwide cooperation policy. In place of a policy of maximum secrecy and non-cooperation, he called for accelerated development of the peaceful uses of atomic energy and worldwide cooperation in this endeavor, including the supply by the advanced nuclear nations of both information and the nuclear materials essential to research and development. Significantly, the Eisenhower proposal abandoned by omission the earlier US position favoring the creation of an international authority to own and operate facilities. Instead, he proposed the creation of an international agency which would allocate material to national programs, under appropriate controls of the agency. The details were left to further negotiations, but the US had in mind a system of international inspection which would detect any diversion from peaceful channels.

The Eisenhower proposal was not simply an altruistic gesture to share US progress in peaceful uses with other countries, nor was it exclusively the reflection of a judgment that the inevitable dispersal of scientific knowledge and technological know-how had made the policy of secrecy obsolete, although both of these elements were present. The motives and objectives of the new policy were complex, including the desire to secure a more receptive international climate for the US nuclear defense program, and the desire to engage the Soviet Union in some sort of dialogue on nuclear issues.

The effect of the Eisenhower proposals, both in domestic and international terms, was to trigger dramatic change in the emphasis given to the development of peaceful uses and in the opportunities for international cooperation in this field. In the US, these changes were reflected in the adoption of the Atomic Energy Act of 1954, which authorized and encouraged the expanded international cooperation. Internationally, the new era was perhaps best typified by the 1955 Geneva Conference on the Peaceful Uses of Atomic Energy, which attracted more than 1,400 participants from some 60 countries, including the Soviet Union and other Eastern European countries, and occasioned the declassification by the leading nuclear countries of a vast accumulation of information of direct importance to peaceful uses of nuclear energy, including nuclear power.

Despite these dramatic changes, concern over the relationship between peaceful uses, especially nuclear power, and the risk of proliferation had by no means come to an end. The new policy specifically called for safeguards to provide assurance against diversion of peaceful nuclear assistance to military purposes. The new US legislation provided for a number of procedural and substantive restraints on cooperation toward the same end. In particular, the legislation required a "guaranty" by each recipient country that it would not use the materials or equipment supplied "for research or development of nuclear weapons, or for any other military purpose." The Atomic Energy Act of 1954 did not require cooperating nations to accept inspections by either US or international inspectors; the decision to take this step was an Executive Branch decision and not a Congressional one.

Procedurally, the new legislation required that, following completion of negotiations, an Agreement for Cooperation be sent to the President for approval, authorization of execution, and a statutory finding. Following this, the agreements were to be submitted to the Joint Committee on Atomic Energy, where they would lie for a period of 30 days before becoming effective. While no explicit Congressional veto was provided for, the purpose of the provision for Congressional review was unmistakable: Congressional objection to an Agreement before it became effective would give the Congress the leverage to exercise strong control, if not a formal veto, over the bilateral agreements.

The earliest bilateral agreements negotiated under the new legislation were for research. These arrangements provided for the transfer of research reactors and their fuel, which was limited in quantity, and in enrichment to no more than 20 percent U^{235}. The fuel was to be provided in fuel element form and returned in the same form. Agreements of this type introduced the principle of inspection by outside authorities by granting to the United States the right "to observe from time to time" the reactor and its fuel. However, the limitations on amount, enrichment, and reprocessing of the fuel basically made these agreements self-safeguarding, i.e., material of strategic significance was simply not made available under the agreements.

The concept of international safeguards came into its own in agreements which were first concluded in 1956, and which provided for cooperation in power reactors. Since these agreements provided for much larger fuel transfers, and for their use in power reactors which would produce substantial amounts of plutonium, much more comprehensive and detailed rights of inspection and control were deemed necessary. The fundamental principle of the new safeguards was to be on-site inspection by outside authorities with broad rights of access and inquiry. The United States was to have the right to send inspectors who would have, in the words of the agreements, "access to all places and data necessary" to account for safeguarded material in order to determine compliance with the agreement.

In addition to the safeguard rights *per se,* these comprehensive agreements contained several other provisions of direct relevance and importance to non-proliferation. Among these were:

1. The US right of approval over the means and location of reprocessing of any US-supplied fuel. (A similar right over fuel of non-US origin irradiated in US-supplied reactors was omitted. This omission was to become an important issue more than 20 years later.)

2. A US right to designate the facilities in which fissionable material produced in excess of the country's peaceful needs was to be stored. Such storage facilities could presumably be located either within or outside the recipient country.

3. An option on behalf of the US to purchase fissionable material produced in excess of the other country's needs in its peaceful program.

These provisions are of major importance in indicating the intention of the parties with respect to reprocessing and plutonium recycle, issues which were also to become the subject of intense debate many years later.

US policy from the outset had been to channel as much cooperation as possible, but not the supply of nuclear materials, through the International Atomic Energy Agency (IAEA) and, in particular, to rely on the Agency to perform the safeguards function. However, establishment of the IAEA involved extended and complex multilateral negotiations, particularly with respect to the safeguards issue. Thus the US proceeded with the conclusion of bilateral power agreements, but incorporated in these arrangements provisions which called for transfer of the safeguards responsibilities to the IAEA when it was in a position to assume them.

In the meantime, the charter, or statute, of the IAEA was under negotiation at the United Nations in New York. Through no coincidence, its safeguard language closely parallels that of the United States bilateral agreements negotiated at the same time. The provision relating to inspection in the IAEA statute is even more explicit than in US bilateral agreements, authorizing access not only to all places and data, but "at all times," and to "all persons." The provision of the IAEA statute relating to reprocessing approval makes it clear that this approval shall be for the sole purpose of ensuring that the facility permits the effective application of safeguards.

The provisions relating to reprocessing and produced material storage have an important bearing on the present non-proliferation debate. Among the contentions of some proponents of a policy of prohibition or restriction of reprocessing and plutonium utilization is that the safeguards regime was adequate for the era of the once-through fuel cycle, but was never intended to be applicable to these higher risk activities. In fact, the provisions of the earliest bilateral power agreements as well as of the Statute of the International Atomic Energy Agency reflect that the safeguards and non-proliferation regime were intended to accommodate reprocessing and the use of plutonium.

Both the US bilateral agreements and the agency statute allow recipient countries to retain the plutonium actually needed in their peaceful programs, placing restrictions only on the means used for chemical processing and on the storage of any surplus, thus clearly anticipating plutonium recycle. While these activities were singled out for special treatment in the safeguards provisions, this detailed treatment prescribed the conditions under which these activities could occur, rather than prohibit them, an intention which could have been expressed much more briefly and clearly, had it been present. The reasons for the special treatment given to reprocessing are discussed later in this section.

The fact that reprocessing and plutonium use were conditioned but not prohibited in early agreements is not surprising. From the outset of the power reactor era, reprocessing and the re-use of plutonium were viewed as natural and desirable parts of the fuel cycle. Reactor economic studies over a period of many years customarily included a credit for spent fuel corresponding to the fuel value of its residual U^{235} and plutonium, less estimated reprocessing and waste disposal charges. This credit — estimated to be a fraction of a mil per kwh — was not insignificant in the economic comparison with conventional power costs, and in the competition among reactor types, which characterized decision making on the selection of power generation systems in the early days of nuclear power. No voices were raised against the presumed use of plutonium; on the contrary, the failure to solve the reprocessing and related waste disposal problem was the subject of frequent criticism by opponents of nuclear power.

C. The IAEA and the Development of Safeguards

Concurrent with the technical presumption that reprocessing and plutonium recycle were an expected part of the light water reactor fuel cycle, technical safeguards studies from the beginning of the Atoms for Peace program were concentrated on how to safeguard effectively the sensitive fuel cycle activities — above all, reprocessing. Early studies indicated that effective safeguarding of large reprocessing plants would require a substantial number of "resident" inspectors located at the facility around-the-clock.

The potential for political difficulty inherent in this requirement was evident from the start. In contrast to the bilateral situation, where the US initiated inspection activities on the basis of the agreement language without further definition, IAEA member states insisted that the Agency formulate a safeguards "system," defining in more detail how the Agency would actually implement safeguards, before agreeing to make the necessary organizational and budgetary provisions for an agency safeguards capability. The Soviet Union took the position that safeguards were another capitalist imposition on the developing countries, and did not require safeguards in its own modest bilateral arrangements.

The US approach was to develop IAEA safeguards on a step by step basis. By confining the initial IAEA safeguards system to small and relatively nonsensitive facilities, the US and its partners hoped to avoid the foreseeably difficult problems associated with the intensive inspection required by larger facilities. It also believed that pacing the development of Agency safeguards to actual needs would be less subject to political attack and more in keeping with technical reality.

In 1960, the Agency adopted its first safeguards system, calling for reports, records, and inspections of increasing frequency on reactors of increasing size up to the limit of 100 MW thermal. The issue of inspection frequency, as anticipated, dominated the debate on this occasion, and inspection frequency or intensity has continued to be the dominant issue in Agency safeguards development to the present time.

The adoption of the limited safeguards system was a breakthrough of sorts, but it did not permit the US to turn to the IAEA in a definitive way for safeguards application on power reactors, which were well over 100 MW thermal rating. Not only were other countries reluctant to accept Agency safeguards of undefined severity, the US was also reluctant to rely upon Agency safeguards which in practice might turn out to be unacceptably lenient.

Nevertheless, in the major safeguards dispute of its day, the US was coming under increasing pressure to redirect its cooperative program from primary reliance on the bilateral route to primary reliance on the IAEA. The Statute of the IAEA authorized it to serve, in effect, as a materials broker, and there is little doubt that the US initially viewed this as one of the Agency's important tasks. Limiting the distribution of nuclear materials to Agency channels would result in nuclear activities in other countries (which by and large were then dependent on US-supplied nuclear materials) becoming Agency-assisted projects, and thus automatically subject to IAEA safeguards. In contrast, when projects were undertaken bilaterally, the application of Agency safeguards was a matter for agreement between the bilateral parties, and the US and other suppliers had not been insisting upon Agency safeguards in these bilateral negotiations.

The criticism of US policy became especially intense with the negotiation of an agreement with the European Atomic Energy Community (Euratom), which omitted even the customary provision authorizing termination in the event of a failure to agree on the transfer of safeguards responsibility to the IAEA, while simultaneously delegating safeguards responsibility under the agreement to Euratom. The charge was made repeatedly that through the policies cited above, the United States was undercutting the Agency which it had created and, in doing so, was jeopardizing the most promising mechanism for bringing proliferation under control.

An unexpected aspect of the situation described above was the strong preference of nearly all recipient countries to rely upon the materials supply arrangements and safeguards administration of the United States, in preference to those of the IAEA. The assumption that countries might resent US inspections on their territory, but would at least tolerate, if not welcome, inspection by an international organization of which they were themselves members was an important element in the US proposal to establish the IAEA. Yet numerous governments informed the United States that they feared that placing the supply of vitally needed energy resource in the hands of an international body would subject supply arrangements to potential political pressure, and that safeguards administration also might be used as a means of harassment or false accusation.

As a result, the voluntary transfer of either fuel supply arrangements or safeguards administration to the IAEA proved virtually impossible, and the US was reluctant to make use of the coercive mechanism of termination provided in some of its bilateral agreements to bring about the transfer. With the notable exception of Japan, which voluntarily requested the application of IAEA safeguards to its bilateral arrangements with the US and other suppliers in the early 60s, no major recipient nation was prepared to accept IAEA safeguards.

For vastly different reasons, a major sector of Congress had expressed reservations from the outset on the supply of US nuclear material through the IAEA. As an international organization, the IAEA was bound by its statute to distribute nuclear material made available to it on a non-discriminatory basis. This meant that US material, once made available for distribution to the IAEA, was no longer under US control, except to the extent that the US, as an Agency member, might influence Agency actions. Some material might even be transferred to Soviet-bloc countries, a prospect which was hardly palatable in the atmosphere of the 1950s.

Against this background, the Administration undertook a fundamental review in 1961 of the respective roles of bilateral agreements and the IAEA in US nuclear cooperation arrangements. The conclusion was that the crucial role for the IAEA was not to serve as a middleman in the distribution of nuclear fuel which it played no part in producing, but rather to be the exclusive agent for the administration of safeguards. To achieve this result, the US recognized that it would have to adopt a far more rigid policy in insisting that nations accept IAEA safeguards as a condition for the supply of US nuclear materials. While the Agency materials distribution role was deemphasized, the US remained ready to supply material through the IAEA when this route was preferable to the recipient.

The reasons for the adoption of this policy — both with respect to the Agency's materials distribution function and its safeguards function — are relevant to certain aspects of the current non-proliferation debate and thus warrant some exploration.

The original conception of the IAEA as a broker or distributor of nuclear materials was that it would mediate claims to a potentially scarce resource, thus relieving the producers of this thankless task, and bringing the consumers collectively into the process of deciding which of their needs would be fulfilled. The reality of the 60s was that both enrichment capacity and uranium were available in such abundance that no need existed for allocation. Thus the Agency's role as a material distributor came to be viewed, at best, as a paper function, and, at worst, as an opportunity for political mischief by withholding supplies from politically unpopular regimes. Whether the Agency would, in fact, have functioned this way, is open to question, but the concerns were sufficiently strong to lead most of its members to prefer direct bilateral relations with producers.

In the United States, proposals have been made recently, both within and outside the government, for the establishment of an international entity capable of providing firm fuel supply assurances that would supplement, and, when necessary, supplant bilateral fuel deliveries. It is essential to the credibility of this approach that the international entity have both the physical capability to make delivery of nuclear fuel, perhaps through the creation of a stockpile located on territory which would be immune to overriding national authority, and the institutional immunity from veto by individual nations. Opposition to this approach is coming from individuals who in the past have been critical of the few arrangements in which the IAEA is acting as distributor of US-supplied fuel. This opposition has been based on the fact that under these arrangements, which are governed by the US-IAEA Agreement for Cooperation, the IAEA and not the US is responsible for determining whether and under what conditions the reprocessing and retransfer of US supplied material may take place.

The unavoidable fact is that the delegation of functions and authority involving the supply of nuclear materials or services to an international entity, diminishes supply control over these areas. It remains to be seen whether the US will be prepared to agree to the control by some international entity — whether the IAEA or some new body — over the disposition of US-supplied nuclear materials, or whether any international body exercising these functions will be willing to relinquish much of its authority over the disposition of the material to the supplying nation.

While uranium enrichment services are capable of being expanded essentially without limitation, uranium supplies are finite, and there is currently concern that the availability of uranium will limit nuclear power expansion through light water reactors around the end of the century. Thus, the need for an international entity to perform the resource allocation function once intended for the IAEA may again become real, regardless of any proliferation consideration. In this instance, too, however, the readiness of recipient countries to accept international decision-making in preference to dependence on direct bilateral relationships with suppliers, even under tight market conditions, is highly uncertain. Much will depend on the specific composition and terms of reference for any international authority conceived for this purpose.

In summary, the function of acting as a broker for the supply of nuclear materials, originally viewed as an important role for the IAEA, proved to be unpopular with both producers — chief among them the US — and recipients, and except in a few special cases, the role never materialized. Suggestions are once again being made that this role be played by some international entity — in part to provide strengthened assurances of nuclear fuel availability so as to deter independent and uncontrolled entry into sensitive fuel cycle areas. The approach may have merit, but past events demonstrate that difficult problems must be overcome before the concept will be acceptable either to suppliers or consumers. Also since private companies, rather than governments tend to be dominant in the exploration, production and ownership of uranium, commercial considerations may make the development of an international uranium resource allocation mechanism extremely unrealistic.

The rationale for the US decision — followed also by other suppliers — to require IAEA safeguards administration as a condition of bilateral supply arrangements is also relevant to the present day proliferation debate. The criticism of the late 1950s and early 1960s that the United States was abandoning or undermining the IAEA by not insisting upon its role as the safeguards authority was characterized by a certain sentimentalism with respect to the merits of international institutions. In fact, as those with responsibility for the development of international safeguards arrangements were well aware, the decision to rely upon an international organization — particularly one where potential recipients who would become subject to safeguards far outnumbered potential suppliers — brought with it considerable risks and difficulties.

Despite the strong US influence in the IAEA — far stronger then than now — it is clear that the US would be unable to prescribe unilaterally the agency safeguards system. Thus, the delegation of responsibility for safeguards administration to the IAEA carried with it a surrender of US control over the nature of the safeguards system and its implementation which could well entail a reduction in effectiveness in comparison with the norm which the US might apply bilaterally. In short, as was pointed out at the time, if the objective of safeguards were only to assure the US that the material and assistance which it supplied was not diverted to military use, then the delegation of safeguards responsibility to an international organization was an irrational way to achieve this objective.

There were, however, other strong practical reasons for transferring safeguards responsibility to the IAEA, despite the apparent unpopularity of this move with most recipient nations. Additional suppliers were present in the international nuclear market from the outset. These and other potential suppliers were reluctant to develop their own independent safeguards capability, and the effectiveness of such capabilities, if established, would in some cases, have been subject to considerable doubt. Competition among suppliers could also give rise to pressures to downgrade safeguards as an inducement to sales. Thus, the need to have effective safeguards not only on the exports of one supplier but equally on all, pointed to the desirability of a uniform international system administered by the IAEA.

In the world community as a whole, bilateral safeguards also suffered from a lack of credibility. The application of safeguards by a supplier nation, such as the United States, to one of its own close partners or allies might satisfy the supplier that diversion was not taking place, but in the eyes of other nations, the arrangement might be viewed simply as a cover for the transfer of a nuclear capability. Here again, the solution appeared to be a uniform safeguards system administered by an agency of broadly based international membership.

Ironically, the first test of the new US policy to require IAEA safeguards as a condition of its bilateral assistance was the negotiation, in 1963, of an agreement with India covering the supply of a nuclear power reactor. India was in the forefront of the nations which contended that safeguards, like supply, should be a bilateral relationship between supplier and recipient. Nevertheless, following intensive negotiations lasting more than a year, agreement was reached under which India accepted IAEA safeguards on the project, subject to certain conditions to be fulfilled in due course. India accepted IAEA safeguards in a trilateral agreement (India-US-IAEA) concluded in 1969, thus bringing the arrangement to the intended conclusion.

In the meantime, IAEA safeguards progressed on two fronts. Suppliers, led by the US, successfully imposed their policy of insisting on IAEA, rather than bilateral, safeguards. Concurrently, the development of the Agency safeguards system was moving forward step by step in Vienna. In 1962, the Agency adopted safeguards for reactors without limitation on size, agreeing for the first time that "access at all times" was appropriate when large facilities were involved. This step in the development of safeguards also saw the adoption of an important principle, "pursuit", on which agreement had been impossible in the earlier system of safeguards for small reactors. "Pursuit" required that safeguards extend not only to material and equipment originally supplied under safeguards, but to all produced fissionable material derived from this material, without limitation on the number of generations. This was an essential step in ensuring the effectiveness of IAEA safeguards.

This round in the development of the IAEA safeguards system was also accompanied by an important political development. For the first time, the Soviet Union gave unqualified support to effective safeguards, a support which was to remain strong and consistent from that time forward.

The next step in the development of IAEA safeguards was perhaps the most difficult and important one. Agreement had been reached on a system of safeguards for reactors of all sizes, but not for reprocessing plants, or other non-reactor facilities handling bulk materials. The Agency Safeguards Committee was convened once again in 1965 and reached agreement on a system of safeguards for reprocessing plants. As anticipated, the principal issue was inspection frequency and intensity. The US and some other suppliers were convinced that the effective safeguarding of reprocessing plants required continuous inspection, and that it was essential, to avoid future controversy, that such inspection be explicitly provided for in the safeguards document. This goal was achieved, although, in a compromise typical of such multilateral negotiations, the provision authorizing continuous access appears in a footnote of the document. The US took the lead in the extension of the system to reprocessing facilities, and, as it had done in the past in connection with reactors, it sought to assist the agency in developing an actual safeguards capability by voluntarily placing its own commercial fuel reprocessing facility (the nuclear fuel services plant in West Valley, N.Y. — since shut down), under IAEA safeguards for an extended safeguards demonstration and development exercise. With this round of negotiations, an agency safeguards system applicable to all steps of the nuclear fuel cycle except enrichment had been formulated.

The development of the Agency safeguards system has major relevance to considerations of non-proliferation policy. The negotiations of safeguards systems and agreements, and the allocation by the IAEA of adequate resources to implement its system effectively has involved a constant effort against strong opposition to limit the intensity of both the system and its implementation. These facts indicate, as might be anticipated, that there is a major gulf between a nation's acceptance of the principle of non-proliferation, and its readiness to accept restraints that it perceives as interference with its ability to pursue the peaceful uses of nuclear energy. Indeed, the tendency is quite the opposite: nations which accept restrictions on their right to engage in military and "peaceful" explosive uses of nuclear energy take the position that they have earned the right to undertake safeguarded nuclear activities without undue restraint, a position which has been incorporated in Article IV of the Non-Proliferation Treaty (see Chapter IV section B, p.76 *et seq.*).

The critical ingredient which enabled IAEA safeguards negotiations to reach a conclusion which the US and a few other safeguard-minded nations were able to accept was the strong leverage the United States derived from its positive contributions to international nuclear cooperation. While explicit trade-offs or threats of withdrawal of nuclear assistance were not employed, the recognition of the US role as a principal supplier of nuclear materials, equipment, and technology, and of the dependence of this role on a satisfactory outcome to the safeguard negotiations, underlay the entire negotiating process. In the face of a numerically overwhelming preference for the least intensive safeguards possible, a strong bargaining position on the part of those nations which favor more effective controls depends on their ability to contribute affirmatively to the development of peaceful uses.

D. The Non-Proliferation Treaty (NPT)

The history of the evolution of IAEA safeguards does not end with the development of the IAEA system described above. The successful negotiation of the Non-Proliferation Treaty gave the Agency a new and more important safeguards role than ever before. It was, under Article III of the Treaty, to apply its safeguards in "all peaceful nuclear activities within the territory of such State. . . . ."

The issue of safeguards was a crucial and difficult one in the negotiation of the NPT. At the outset, the Euratom member states were reluctant to consider accepting IAEA safeguards in any form, insisting that their own regional system should meet any reasonable need for verification. This exception was quickly found to be unacceptable to the Soviet Union and other non-Euratom nations, and for a time, serious consideration was given to proceeding with a non-proliferation treaty in which there was no mechanism for verification of non-proliferation undertakings. The impasse was broken by an understanding that the Euratom states would be allowed to negotiate a safeguards agreement with the IAEA collectively, which presumably would take account of Euratom's multinational safeguards capabilities.

The safeguards issue was not resolved by this development, however. A number of non-nuclear weapon countries, especially such industrially advanced nations as Germany and Japan, expressed the view that safeguards would place them at a commercial and economic disadvantage in pursuing peaceful uses of nuclear energy. The NPT is inherently discriminatory in denying explosive applications of nuclear energy to non-nuclear weapon states, while preserving this opportunity for the existing weapon states. While many countries were prepared to accept this discrimination, which is the essence of "non-proliferation," they were unwilling to see this discrimination extended to the peaceful uses. The insistence on the inclusion in the treaty of a requirement to verify the non-proliferation undertaking by a system of safeguards was particularly distasteful to many non-nuclear weapon states. Universal application of safeguards to all NPT parties might have materially facilitated and accelerated the negotiation of the treaty. The Soviet Union, however, consistent with its traditional opposition to inspection was unwilling to accept safeguards on its own peaceful program. To break what threatened to be a deadlock in the negotiation of the treaty, the US and the UK announced in December 1967 their readiness to place their own peaceful programs under IAEA safeguards.

This was a necessary but not a sufficient condition to secure the agreement of the industrialized non-nuclear weapon states to the treaty as a whole and its safeguards provisions in particular. These countries, and especially the Federal Republic of Germany, argued that the Agency system developed to date was inappropriate to the new circumstances of the NPT. The existing system was based on the assumption that individual projects or groups of projects in a given country would become subject to IAEA safeguards either as the result of Agency assistance to such projects, or agreement of bilateral partners to make use of Agency safeguards. Under the NPT, in contrast, a country's entire peaceful nuclear program would be placed under Agency safeguards.

A number of nations took the position that this fact would permit a more efficient safeguards system, since the opportunities for cross-checking in the fuel cycle would be enhanced. Germany, in particular, argued that improved and less intrusive safeguards could be developed through increased reliance on instrumentation and other technical developments, and by more careful concentration of safeguards efforts at the so-called "strategic points" of the fuel cycle. These principles were accepted in the language of the treaty itself and an understanding was reached that a revised Agency safeguards system, applicable to NPT Parties, would be developed after the treaty entered into force. In signing the treaty, the Euratom member states and Japan conditioned their ratification, among other factors, on satisfaction with the new safeguard arrangements.

To fulfill this understanding, the IAEA Safeguards Committee was reconvened in 1970. It undertook a comprehensive review of the IAEA system, for purposes of its application to NPT parties, following the principles set forth in the NPT. The result does not in any sense represent a wholesale departure from the earlier safeguards document, but rather a tighter, more detailed and somewhat more restrictive set of standards. Once again, the issue of inspection frequency and intensity was paramount, and, once again, strenuous efforts were required to preserve what, in the US view, was adequate inspection effort. The negotiations demonstrated anew that countries would not easily accept strict controls over their peaceful nuclear activities.

E. The Non-Proliferation Regime

With the conclusion of the NPT, which was opened for signature on July 1, 1968, and became effective on March 5, 1970, and with the adoption of the IAEA safeguard system for NPT parties in 1971, the basic institutional arrangements for dealing with the proliferation risks of peaceful nuclear activities were in place. The task of securing maximum adherence to the NPT, especially by countries viewed as most capable of undertaking military nuclear programs continued, as it does to the present time.

The era of international nuclear cooperation which began in 1954 and extended through the events described above, until perhaps 1974, was not without its sharp controversies. As already indicated, these included a dispute over the relative emphasis to be given bilateral as opposed to international or multilateral forms of cooperation, and, especially, safeguards; intense disagreements over the US posture toward Euratom as against the IAEA; and continuing efforts to develop and maintain the effectiveness of IAEA safeguards against the less-than-enthusiastic attitudes of most potential recipient nations. Nevertheless, this was a period of relative consensus, both domestically and internationally, on fundamental principles. The consensus was that peaceful nuclear development could take place with the risk of proliferation at an acceptable level under a system of international safeguards designed to detect, and thereby deter, any violations of peaceful use undertakings. Violations were believed to be unlikely, and there was an unspoken assumption that if they occurred, they would prove to be unacceptable to the world community.

National nuclear development and international nuclear cooperation, as a result, moved ahead during this period at a pace largely determined by technical, economic, environmental, and, above all, commercial considerations, without significant restraint imposed in the name of non-proliferation.

F. Renewed Concerns

The consensus began to weaken in the early 1970s, but the turning point was the Indian nuclear explosion of May 1974. On this occasion, for the first time, a nation exploded a nuclear device built with material derived from assistance which it had obtained from abroad for peaceful purposes. India made no secret of the fact — nor could it — that the plutonium employed in this device was produced in the Cirus 40 MW heavy water moderated research reactor, provided by Canada, and initially charged with heavy water provided by the United States.

There were many special circumstances surrounding the Indian nuclear explosion which makes it less than a convincing test of the adequacy of prevailing non-proliferation policies. The Cirus reactor, as well as its original heavy water, had been obtained by India from Canada and the US under very early arrangements which preceded the development of the clear-cut safeguards policies and arrangements described earlier. The arrangements included an Indian undertaking to use the reactor and heavy water only for peaceful purposes, but these undertakings were not subject to verification by any kind of inspection arrangements. India contended that the explosion was for peaceful purposes only and, therefore, was not in violation of this undertaking.

The United States had informed India in 1970 that such a contention would be unacceptable to the United States. By the time of the Indian explosion, however, India's own production of heavy water had exceeded the amount originally provided by the US, thus introducing a further ambiguity into the question of whether there had been any violation by India of its undertaking to the US. Canada informed India of a similar position, but India felt that it was justified in its contention that its undertakings did not preclude the development of nuclear explosives designated for peaceful purposes.

Even if the undertaking of the Indian arrangement were no different, there is little doubt that the issue of India's freedom to develop a nuclear explosive for peaceful purposes would have been faced long before the explosion occurred if safeguards had been available to signal the diversion of material to a questionable use. While the outcome of the issue can only now be speculated upon, it would clearly have been resolved under far different circumstances than those presented by the *fait accompli* of the May 1974 explosion.

It is, nevertheless, clear that one of the major shortcomings of early bilateral agreements for cooperation, as well as the IAEA statute itself, is the failure to include explicitly so-called "peaceful nuclear explosive devices" in the prohibition against military use which these instruments contain. (An attempt was later made, in February 1975, to correct this lacuna by a pronouncement of the IAEA Director General.)

While the Indian nuclear explosive of 1974 is identified as the principal event which triggered intense and widespread renewed interest in the issue of non-proliferation and safeguards, it is clear that other factors were at work as well. In 1974, President Nixon, while on a visit to the Middle East, offered bilateral agreements for the supply of power reactor facilities to both Egypt and Israel.

The sale of US nuclear reactors to Israel, for possible use in desalination of sea water as well as electric power generation, had been a topic of long-standing interest in the US, and had been discussed on several occasions with Congressional committees. However, the offer of nuclear facilities to both Egypt and Israel, made in the course of what was widely believed in the US to be a trip motivated by the domestic political problems of the President, and at a time when the President's prestige was at a low ebb, raised immediate and vocal protests in the Congress and elsewhere. The view was widely held that nuclear facilities were being offered to achieve political goals, both international and domestic, and that the Middle East was too sensitive a region to risk introduction of even peaceful nuclear facilities.

The facts that the arrangements had been carefully considered in advance, and that they provided that no sensitive parts of the fuel cycle or strategic nuclear material would be present in either Egypt or Israel, did little to overcome the outcry. The result was the passage of legislation which required the submission of Agreements for Cooperation to the Congress under a new procedure which provided the Congress with an explicit opportunity to veto any such agreements by majority vote and without provision for Presidential override. This unmistakable rebuke was clear indication of growing Congressional concern over President Nixon's offer as well as non-proliferation policy.

Another new factor in the non-proliferation equation was the concern over the risks of terrorism. The international safeguards system whose development was described earlier in this chapter was directed principally toward the possibility of national diversion or the abrogation of non-proliferation undertakings. To the extent that the issue of subnational diversion or terrorism had been considered at all in the international context, the presumption was that this was the responsibility of individual nations to avoid or control, and the IAEA Statute gave the Agency no explicit power to apply or set standards for protective measures against subnational actions.

Concern that nuclear materials might be stolen by individuals for profit or other motivations was not new. However, the rise of terrorism in the early 70s led to suggestions that nuclear material or facilities might become the target for terrorist attacks. In particular, the proposition was persuasively advanced that a technically competent individual or small group, relying only on information already available in the public domain, could success-fully convert seized plutonium to crude atomic explosives within a matter of days or even hours, depending on the extent of prior preparation of the non-nuclear components of the device.

The intense public and congressional interest generated by this issue had a profound impact on US nuclear developments, both domestic and interna-tional. Among other consequences, it led to immediate moves to strengthen US physical security arrangements, and to the decision that plutonium recy-cle, the desirability of which had scarcely been questioned up till then, should be deferred pending the preparation of an environmental impact statement which would emphasize the safeguards and security aspects of the use of large quantities of separated plutonium. Perhaps as much as any other development, this initiated the chain of events which has led to the 1977 US decisions on indefinite deferral of reprocessing and recycle, and deemphasis of the plutonium breeder.

Important as it is in its own right, the issue of terrorism and other forms of subnational diversion or theft of nuclear material does not involve prolifera-tion as that term is ordinarily understood. The distinction is not an artificial or formal one. Terrorist threats to nuclear material are of a different nature and are susceptible to much different forms of protection than are the risks of governmental diversion and national proliferation. Moreover, gov-ernments possess both resources and virtually unlimited authority, including police power, to counter subnational threats, while the risks of national diversion must be dealt with through the relatively limited tools of diplo-macy, sanctions, and international institutions. While the problem of ter-rorism and physical security is properly receiving continuing attention, the risk of proliferation in the traditional sense is increasingly being recognized as the greater and perhaps more intractable risk.

In addition to these specific events and developments, less tangible factors also undoubtedly played a role in the resurgence of the non-proliferation is-sue. The 1970s, especially in the United States, were characterized by de-clining confidence in the "establishment" and by rising public demands for participation in the decision-making process. Of particular relevance to the proliferation issue was the rapid development of the environmental move-ment and its sharp focus on nuclear power. Environmental organizations as-sumed a leading role in the criticism of non-proliferation policy.

A further factor of major importance in the revival of the proliferation de-bate has been the spread, at an earlier date than most had anticipated, of nuclear power in general, and sensitive fuel cycle activities in particular, to countries or regions which, rightly or wrongly, tend to be viewed as poten-tially less stable. The sales of reprocessing and other sensitive facilities to Pakistan, Brazil, and Korea and the discussions of similar arrangements with Iran, falling on already fertile soil of discontent with US nuclear coop-eration policies, had an immediate and profound effect, both on US Execu-tive Branch policy and Congressional attitudes, now reflected in the 1978 Non-Proliferation Act. Their concern has been directed toward a spectrum

of proliferation risks, the technical aspects of which are described in detail in
Appendix A. The legislative basis for US non-proliferation policy, including
an analysis of the policies, purposes and responsibilities set out in the 1978
Non-Proliferation Act, is found in Volume II, Appendix B.

IV. INSTITUTIONAL OBSTACLES TO PROLIFERATION

The concern that engaging in peaceful uses of nuclear energy would increase the risk of proliferation of nuclear weapons has given rise to a unique
set of policies, arrangements, and institutions designed to allow the widespread enjoyment of the benefits of nuclear energy without unacceptable
proliferation risks. Most of the components of the currently existing non-
proliferation regime have been described in general terms in the preceding
historical account. In the following chapter, they are reviewed briefly, together with background information of relevance to the current debate on
non-proliferation policy.

A. Safeguards and the IAEA

Safeguards are both the most distinctive element of the non-proliferation
regime and one of the most controversial. It is likely that they constitute the
most misunderstood facet of the system. Safeguards, in the meaning which
has been given to the term in non-proliferation usage, are measures designed
to detect, by objective technical means, diversions of nuclear materials from
authorized peaceful uses to unauthorized purposes. In the positive, and
hopefully more normal case, safeguards constitute a means to verify that undertakings to limit nuclear activities to peaceful purposes are being fulfilled.
The central feature of the safeguards system is actual on-site inspection,
conducted by technically qualified international civil servants on the staff of
the International Atomic Energy Agency, if nuclear activities are subject to
safeguards. The inspections are not confined to "accounting" or "book-
keeping" but include actual physical surveillance of activities where material could be diverted, and measures for containment of material within
agreed boundaries.

The concept that international obligations should be subjected to independent verification is a novel one in international relations, and its applications
in the field of non-proliferation can be viewed as a development of potential
importance in other fields. On-site verification has long been regarded as essential to certain types of arms control arrangements with the Soviet Union,
but agreement on such measures has never been ratified, and the arms control arrangements between the nuclear super powers have, therefore, so far
been limited to those which are susceptible to "national verification", i.e.,
to measures undertaken by each party without intrusion into the territory of
the other party.

The fact that the IAEA safeguards system is one for the detection of violations, or the verification of undertakings, and not a system which possesses
the police power to prevent violations, to enforce obligations, or to punish
offenses has been made clear from the outset of the Atoms for Peace pro-

75

gram. The view has always been that the risk of detection would deter violations, and that if violations did occur, safeguards would trigger appropriate
sanctions. Neither are safeguards a system of physical protection designed
to prevent subnational seizure of nuclear material. However, the verification
measures employed in the safeguards system are equally capable of detecting diversions regardless of whether they are nationally or subnationally directed, even though the primary intent of the system is to verify national
compliance with, or to detect national violation of, peaceful undertakings.

With increasing awareness of the nature of safeguards, the controversy
concerning them has shifted to new ground. A key element — perhaps the
single most important one — in the position of those who advocate restrictions or prohibition of reprocessing and plutonium utilization is that
these activities cannot be safeguarded effectively since diverted material
could be transformed into nuclear explosives within a matter of days or
hours, before countermeasures could be applied or the underlying national
security problem which gave rise to the violation corrected. It will be seen
from what has been said of the nature of safeguards that this criticism, to the
extent that it is valid, is not a criticism of safeguards, but of the steps which
are expected to occur after safeguards have played their role of detection of
diversion.

The concern which may be validly directed toward safeguards is whether
the system itself possesses the technical capability for the prompt detection
of the diversion of significant amounts (i.e., strategic quantities) of weapon-
usable material, and whether the application of the system is sufficiently
vigorous for this capability to be realized in practice. These concerns are of
direct relevance to the current issues of reprocessing, plutonium recycle,
and the breeder.

B. The Non-Proliferation Treaty

The Non-Proliferation Treaty has occupied a position of central importance both in the development of the existing non-proliferation regime
and in the current controversy surrounding it. While the Treaty has a
number of motivations, its principal purpose and virtue in terms of the current issues is its role in "filling the gap" left by the earlier policies of requiring peaceful use undertakings and safeguards on exports of nuclear assistance. So long as countries remained dependent on outside sources for nuclear materials and equipment, and so long as the suppliers of these items
required peaceful undertakings and safeguards on them as a condition of
their export, peaceful nuclear activities would become subject to the non-
proliferation regime.

In fact, to a very large degree, this is the situation which has prevailed up
to the present time. In virtually every country except the nuclear weapon
states themselves, but including countries such as West Germany and Japan,
which have substantial indigenous nuclear industrial capabilities, all or
nearly all significant nuclear activities have become subject to peaceful use

undertakings as a result of requirements placed upon nuclear exports by the suppliers of facilities or materials to these countries. To a large extent, the worldwide use of light water reactors, fueled with enriched uranium until recently available in commercial quantities only from the US, has been responsible for this state of affairs. However, other reactor suppliers — the UK, Canada, West Germany, and, for a number of years, the Soviet Union — have followed similar policies, with the result that with only a few exceptions (for example, the Dimona reactor in Israel, the Cirus reactor in India and the Vandellos reactor in Spain) both safeguards and peaceful use undertakings are applicable to all existing significant nuclear activities in non-nuclear weapon states.

Nevertheless, as has been observed, an increasing number of countries are developing the capability to undertake significant nuclear activities. At the same time, a growing number of countries have reached the stage where they are able to act as nuclear suppliers, and not all may follow the non-proliferation policies of the existing supplier states. The NPT fills the gap of indigenous nuclear programs, or programs which depend on imports from countries that do not require safeguards, by providing a mechanism for countries to agree not to acquire nuclear explosives in any way, and to allow verification of this undertaking by placing all of their peaceful nuclear activities under IAEA safeguards.

The NPT has long been regarded in the United States as the principal non-proliferation tool, and US national policy has been to encourage the widest possible adherence to the Treaty. The efforts have been met with considerable success: 102 nations, including virtually all of the world's major industrialized nations (except France, already a nuclear weapon state) are now parties to the Treaty. A number of so-called threshold countries — those with both a technical capability, and a possible incentive to acquire nuclear weapons — have remained outside. These include certain pairs or groups of countries: Israel and some Arab nations, India and Pakistan, Brazil and Argentina being the principal examples.

C. Bilateral Restraints and Export Policy

While the basic principle of non-proliferation policy since 1953, both for the US and other potential suppliers, has been one of cooperation under controls, the policy has not placed total reliance on the effectiveness of safeguards. Elements of restraint and denial have also been present from the start. However, both the nature of these additional controls and their rationale are frequently misunderstood.

Among the most significant of these controls was the exclusion of enrichment technology or facilities from the area of permissible cooperation. Since US reactor technology depends on the use of enriched uranium (more than it is dependent on reprocessing) an argument could be made, and indeed has been made by other nations, that an open-handed policy of cooperation could have included access to US enrichment technology. The US position, which has been followed by other enrichers as well, is that enrichment technology is directly relevant to military applications, and thus too sensitive to disclose. This same argument could be applied to reprocessing technology, and for a period of time, this was in fact the case. The original US declassification of reprocessing technology did not take place until the Geneva conference of 1958, although earlier exchanges with other countries on a classified basis had already occurred.

The reasons for the different treatment ultimately decided upon for reprocessing and enrichment are not easily discerned. Certainly one factor may have been the long standing belief that the gaseous diffusion process represented a technological achievement of such a unique nature that it was unlikely to be duplicated. Reprocessing, in contrast, while viewed as an important development, was generally recognized as relying upon relatively conventional chemical technology. Another factor may well have been that since the US held itself out as prepared to meet all requirements for enriched uranium, it saw no need to grant access to its technology. It was not in a similar position to give assurances as to the availability of reprocessing services, although there is no doubt that at one time there was an intention to become a supplier of these services, and thus inhibit their spread to other countries.

While the US chose to make enrichment services available, it did not seek to restrain their development elsewhere by explicit agreement provisions. US bilateral agreements left open the possibility that US-supplied reactors could be fueled with other than US-enriched uranium, and enrichment supply agreements entered into under the bilaterals specifically gave the user the right to terminate the agreement if he wished to make use of another source of supply.

These facts are indicative of a deliberate policy which characterized US nuclear cooperation arrangements from an early date: efforts to discourage the development of independent, and potentially proliferation-prone sources of sensitive fuel cycle services abroad were based principally on the positive feature of offering dependable supply on attractive terms from the US rather than on seeking specific prohibitions against these activities. Indeed, the most significant example of this approach is the basic principle that only the materials and equipment specifically exported under the agreement would be subject to peaceful use undertakings and safeguards. The recipient nation remained free to undertake independent nuclear programs — civil or military — outside the restraints of the agreement if it chose to do so — as did France, for example. The US approach was to create disincentives for such activities through favorable supply arrangements, but not to seek to prohibit them.

Clearly, it would have been possible to seek total prohibition of military nuclear activities as a *quid pro quo* for US assistance in peaceful uses. The extent to which this approach was considered is not a matter of public knowledge, and whether it would have been acceptable to other nations, if tried, can only be speculated upon.

New approaches now under consideration in the US would reverse this policy, and would make eligibility for certain new fuel cycle assurances specifically dependent upon the other nation's agreement to refrain from such activities as reprocessing, enrichment, and plutonium utilization on a national basis. The acceptability of this approach under current circumstances remains to be determined.

US policy and agreements contained other restraints besides the exclusion of enrichment cooperation. Of particular importance to the current debate were the provisions relating to reprocessing, storage of produced material and purchase of produced material. In early nuclear agreements, the US had the unqualified right to approve reprocessing or any other alterations of irradiated fuel. It also had the right to designate the facilities for storage of produced fissionable material in excess of the other country's needs for its peaceful program, and to buy this excess at published prices. (Under the Atomic Energy Act of 1954, the US government was obliged to purchase plutonium from domestic licensees.)

The effect of these provisions was to allow recipient countries to retain, or to have returned to them, any produced plutonium which they required for their peaceful programs. The provisions relating to storage and buy back, while sufficiently broad in language to accommodate produced material in separated form, were designed to apply to unseparated plutonium. Thus, while these provisions show a clear intent to single out reprocessing and plutonium as special proliferation hazards, they also reflect a decision to control, but not to prohibit these activities.

As observed earlier, the language of the IAEA statute, negotiated during the same time period, is even more explicit, making the Agency's right of approval of reprocessing dependent solely on the determination that safeguards can be effectively applied in the facility in question. As time went on, the provisions of the US bilateral agreements were brought more nearly into line with those of the IAEA statute. The US options to purchase excess produced material, never exercised, began to be omitted from amended agreements in the mid-1960s. The reprocessing provision took on several different forms, but the criterion of safeguardability became, if not the sole, then at least the principal test for US agreement to reprocessing abroad.

Closely related to these agreement provisions concerning reprocessing was US policy on the supply of reprocessing plants, equipment, and technology. One of the important early actions following initiation of the Atoms for Peace program was the decision to limit drastically the effect of the sweeping prohibition of the Atomic Energy Act against participating "directly or indirectly" in the production of fissionable material abroad. The language of this provision of the Act, which was present in the 1946 version and was carried forward to the 1954 legislation, was so broad as to raise questions even regarding such activities as teaching nuclear physics to foreign students in US universities. To overcome the difficulty, a general authorization was issued in 1956 to engage in such activities so long as they did not involve the transfer of classified information or the export of controlled facilities or material. The effect of this general authorization, which did not exclude reprocessing (after the 1958 declassification), was to permit the transfer of peaceful nuclear technology to all but Soviet bloc countries, leaving the export of materials and equipment as the mechanism for triggering the application of safeguards and peaceful use undertakings.

This action was consistent with a long held attitude, by no means confined to the atomic energy program, that the control of information (unless specifically classified) not only presented enormous administrative problems in the US system, but was offensive to traditional US attitudes with respect to the transmission of ideas. The Atomic Energy Act of 1954, in fact, deprived the US Atomic Energy Commission of any authority to limit or control the publication of unclassified information. Thus, from 1958 onward, when reprocessing technology was largely declassified, there was no formal prohibition for a number of years against the transmittal of reprocessing technology. Nevertheless, serious reservations as to the desirability of participating in the construction of reprocessing facilities abroad did exist, and these were translated into informal and ultimately formal restraints.

The basis for these concerns is relevant to present-day issues. As has been observed, US policy contemplated not the prohibition of reprocessing, but its careful control. There was serious concern from the beginning as to whether effective technical safeguards could be designed for reprocessing plants (i.e., safeguards capable of prompt detection of diversion) and, if so, whether safeguards as intense as these were expected to be would be internationally acceptable.

The second concern related to the technical nature of reprocessing technology and facilities. Unlike reactors and uranium enrichment, which involve unique materials and devices, reprocessing plants can be constructed of essentially conventional equipment of the type found in many chemical plants. For this reason, officials from a number of countries concerned with non-proliferation policy doubted whether a reprocessing plant could be defined in such a way as to place effective controls on its export. Thus, if reprocessing technology were exported, the resulting plants would, unlike reactors, not themselves be subject to international safeguards. This meant that while safeguarded nuclear fuel — for example, from a safeguarded reactor — would be safeguarded while undergoing reprocessing in such a plant, the same facility could be used in reprocessing unsafeguarded fuel, leading to the production of unsafeguarded plutonium. This is precisely what occurred in the case of the Indian reprocessing plant at Trombay.

Aware of these difficulties, US officials in the mid-1960s informally deferred the export of US reprocessing technology, taking the position that such export would be appropriate only if the reprocessing plant itself, and not simply fuel from safeguarded reactors, were subject to safeguards. This position was formalized in 1972 by amendments to the appropriate United States regulation (10CFR Part 110, now Part 810) which withdrew the general authorization for transfer of unclassified technology in three sensitive areas — reprocessing, enrichment and heavy water production — and instituted a requirement for specific authorization for cooperation in these areas. A number of criteria for considering proposed cooperation were specified, a principal one being whether the recipient country was an NPT party. Not only would adherence to the NPT ensure that a reprocessing facility, if supplied, be subject to safeguards, but cooperation in this area — if unavailable to non-NPT parties — would provide a positive incentive for countries to become NPT members.

The 1972 amendments to 10 CFR Part 110, with their elaborate criteria for judging proposals for cooperation in reprocessing and the other sensitive areas, make it clear once again that the US policy was not one of prohibition — such a policy could have been expressed in far simpler terms — but rather one of tight control. The distinction is an important one, reflecting again the conclusion that reprocessing was not viewed as an uncontrollable and therefore unacceptable part of the fuel cycle, but as an activity to be surrounded with special precautions in view of its proliferation hazards.

Agreements for the export of reprocessing technology and facilities were entered into by France and West Germany in 1974, after strong objections were raised to these arrangements on non-proliferation ground by the US. In its arrangement with the Republic of Korea for the transfer of a small reprocessing facility, France insisted on a requirement for the application of safeguards not only to the transferred facility itself, but to any facility built by the recipient country for a number of years to come employing the same physical or chemical principle. Applied to the case of reprocessing plants, for example, this meant that any plant based on the solvent extraction process, built by a nation receiving French reprocessing technology, would become subject to IAEA safeguards.

This approach appears to have overcome the earlier concerns that the attachment of safeguards to technology was impractical by adopting a formula where the burden of proof as to the origin of technology could be easily met. At the same time, the approach had another major non-proliferation benefit. It meant that countries which might already be at the threshold of being able to acquire unsafeguarded sensitive facilities through their own efforts might have all such facilities brought under control by application of this requirement. Both France and West Germany have argued that this non-proliferation benefit could, at least in selected cases of countries capable of constructing their own facilities, outweigh the proliferation risk attendant on assisting a country to acquire a reprocessing or other sensitive facility.

Providing reprocessing capability to a country which is unlikely to be able to develop a capability on its own for some time to come may well involve an unnecessary proliferation risk. However, where a country possesses the near-term capability for achieving an indigenous and uncontrolled capability, the position that all reprocessing is undesirable and should be prohibited leaves a disturbing gap. It raises an issue which has been central to non-proliferation policy formulation from the start; whether policies of denial contribute to, or deter, proliferation.

There is a general consensus that proliferation has progressed considerably more slowly than suggested by most forecasts in the early post-war era. At the same time, there is a widely held belief that the Atoms for Peace program has led to a more rapid diffusion of nuclear technology than would have occurred otherwise; indeed, diffusion of peaceful nuclear technology was an avowed objective of the program. Whether the program has substantially increased the number of countries which would otherwise possess the relatively limited amount of knowledge needed to produce small quantities of weapon-usable material is not apparent.

Assuming, nevertheless, that the program has had this effect, the apparent correlation between the policy of cooperation and the encouragingly limited extent of proliferation merits careful consideration. Cooperation in peaceful uses under controls, has made it possible to remove the cloak of legitimacy from uncontrolled national nuclear efforts, and has contributed to the development of a world consensus that the acquisition of nuclear weapons is an undesirable and illegitimate goal. Against this background, the possibility that severe restraints on cooperation will help legitimize unsafeguarded national nuclear efforts cannot be dismissed.

D. Supply Assurances and Other Incentives

The non-proliferation regime which has prevailed since the mid-1950s has always rested on the two-fold foundation of positive incentives and controls. Chief among the incentives offered to deter proliferation pressures have been the assurances of supply of nuclear fuel, facilities, and services.

The concept of assured supply is fundamental. Supply alone, on an *ad hoc* basis, unaccompanied by assurances of its dependability on reasonable terms, would not have had the intended deterrent effect on the development of independent and potentially uncontrolled sources of nuclear materials and equipment. In normal markets, this assurance is supplied largely by the traditions of the market itself, and the self-interest of the supplier in maintaining his profitable supply arrangements. In the case of nuclear materials and equipment, the security sensitivity of the products, the absence of any orderly market tradition and the limited number of suppliers combined to make a new form of governmentally assured supply essential, if the objective of deterring independent sources was to be realized.

As the only source of large amounts of enriched uranium, the US deliberately evolved and pursued a policy of providing this material on the basis of assured availability, designed to deter the development of independent sources of supply. The goal was a difficult one, running counter to the natural tendency of other nations — even before the oil crisis of 1973-74 — to avoid dependence for major proportions of their energy supply upon a single foreign source of supply. The goal was further complicated by the fact that the benefits of nuclear power were not wholly dependent on the use of enriched uranium. Natural uranium is available from a number of sources, and natural uranium power reactors preceded enriched uranium light water reactors to the international marketplace. Despite economic disadvantages, natural uranium reactors remained, and continue to remain, available to nations seeking to avoid the use of enriched uranium.

The US objective of deterring the development of independent sources of enrichment supply was successful for an extended period. This success was achieved through a deliberate policy of making enriched uranium (later, only enrichment services) available on the basis of long-term contractual arrangements involving attractive and nondiscriminatory prices identical to those applicable to domestic users.

Nevertheless, in the late 1960s the US monopoly began to erode. Well before the oil crisis made reduced energy dependence a high priority goal of virtually every nation, and well before mid-1974 when the US abruptly terminated its enrichment contracting when its enrichment capacity became fully booked, both Urenco and Eurodif were conceived and largely committed.

During the same time period, the Soviet Union began vigorous efforts to sell enrichment services, particularly in Western Europe and made considerable headway in this regard as confidence in the US supply began to decline.

The reasons for the decay of the US position after a number of years of successful domination of the enrichment services market is an important topic which merits detailed review. The results, however, speak for themselves; independent sources of supply did emerge. The conclusion is inescapable that the conditions or disadvantages associated with complete reliance on US supply were finally viewed by consumers as excessive. Atomic energy officials of other countries generally confirm this conclusion, and state that the US monopoly could have been maintained much longer, if not indefinitely, had the restrictions, growing uncertainties, and stiffening terms of US enrichment supply been avoided.

Developments in 1974 and later further undermined the credibility of the US supply role, and removed any doubt that the independent sources of enrichment already launched in Europe would go forward. Chief among these developments was the establishment of new institutional responsibilities for US nuclear export licensing, coupled with the emergence of a belief that US nuclear export licenses, even under valid Agreements for Cooperation, could and should be conditioned on the customer's acceptance of new non-proliferation restraints not incorporated in the applicable Agreements.[1]

The long-accepted belief that the US supply monopoly could make an important contribution to the achievement of non-proliferation objectives has recently been subjected to criticism. Complaints that the attachment of new non-proliferation conditions to existing supply commitments was undermining the credibility of these arrangements has been met with the response that this demonstrated the incompatibility of strong supply assurances and non-proliferation leverage. The argument has been made that if the leverage is

---

[1]Richard L. Garwin (United States) adds: The credibility of the US supply role, in my experience and opinion, was mostly undermined by the very strong push of the Nixon Administration toward "privatization" (or give-away) of the enrichment capability. It was at least in part to create an assured market for the product of the private firm that the "shortage" was fostered.

used, it no longer exists, while if not used, in the achievement of non-proliferation objectives, it is illusory.

This argument is somewhat overstated. The expenditure of the US supply leverage unilaterally to impose non-proliferation measures which were not part of the original arrangements was never contemplated, and has undermined US supply credibility without, in many cases, having accomplished its objective. The use of the US leverage to encourage full compliance with agreed non-proliferation undertakings is a far different matter. Neither the affected country nor interested third countries with US supply commitments could complain that this use of leverage was improper, or that it cast doubt on the credibility of US assurances in general. Finally, there is little doubt that, even without explicit exercise of leverage, the existence of a supply relationship involving a major portion of a country's energy needs exercises a restraining influence on any tendency to engage in activities that would be inconsistent with the basic purposes of the arrangement. (For example, the very existence of the strong dependency of many industrialized countries on Middle Eastern oil places certain limits on policies which these countries can follow without jeopardizing the continuity of their petroleum supplies.)

In recent months, the importance of supply assurances and other incentives to the acceptance of non-proliferation restraints has been recognized anew. US legislation has endorsed the extension of firm supply assurances to nations which cooperate with US non-proliferation policies. The US government is considering a variety of arrangements, in addition to assurance of fuel supply, including the storage of spent fuel. Suggestions have been made for a three-tiered system to strengthen fuel supply assurances. This would involve bilateral arrangements as the principal supply mechanism. These bilateral assurances would be backed up by secondary fuel supply arrangements with alternate suppliers, to take effect in the event the primary supply contract were interrupted for reasons unrelated to violation of non-proliferation undertakings. As a final assurance, an international organization could be created with the authority to stockpile and distribute enriched uranium to countries which are in compliance with their non-proliferation undertakings, but whose bilateral supply arrangements have been interrupted for other reasons.

These complex arrangements may help deter the further spread of independent enrichment and reprocessing capabilities. The fact that it has become necessary to devise and consider such arrangements, however, is a disturbing indication of the extent to which the credibility of bilateral fuel supply assurances, once held in high esteem, has been eroded.

Supply of nuclear fuel and fuel cycle services from foreign sources, even if totally reliable, involves foreign exchange expenditures which many nations wish to avoid. This disadvantage may be offset, in part, by economies of scale available through the concentration of fuel cycle activities in a relatively few locations, or by special incentives offered by supplier countries. In the long run, however, the stability of a system which imposes restraints on peaceful nuclear activities which are deemed by cooperating countries to be inconsistent with their political, security or economic interests, may be limited. It is just such restraints which the NPT was designed to avoid.

V. THE DYNAMICS OF THE RELATIONSHIP BETWEEN NUCLEAR POWER PRODUCTION AND NUCLEAR WEAPONS PROLIFERATION

An evaluation of the incremental effect of the development of nuclear power worldwide on the prospects for additional proliferation can be focused in two areas:
 (1) Increased potential for direct production of weapons material;
 (2) Increased potential for diversion of weapons material.

A. The International Environment

The impact of the advance of technology worldwide has been felt strongly and visibly in the development and manufacture of sophisticated weapons systems. Advances in physics, computer technology, communications, materials, aeronautics and space science have all contributed greatly to the ability to create systems for defense and destruction. It is in this context of a highly technological environment that we measure the potential impact of nuclear power on weapons proliferation.

Because of the widespread availability of technology information, it is a question only of decision, time and investment for a nation to develop nuclear weapons. As the technical sophistication of the nation increases, the time and cost of the acquisition of weapons decreases. Almost 50 nations have the minimum facilities, such as a research reactor, required to begin development of a weapons capability leading to a small weapons production program.

It is not simply the development of nuclear power that directly affects the potential for proliferation, since without reprocessing such development is no more threatening than the current large number of research reactors. In the same sense, the worldwide availability of uranium does little to enhance the prospects for proliferation without the capability to enrich such materials to weapon-grade levels. Control of the materials, facilities, and technology associated with uranium enrichment and spent fuel reprocessing is the key to the interface between nuclear power and the acquisition of nuclear weapons materials.

The relationship of the continued development of nuclear power and weapons proliferation depends upon the capabilities and objectives of the nation seeking weapons. With a sovereign nation deliberately planning a weapons program, the direct production route is the preferred way in terms of time and costs. However, the availability of reprocessing capability or enrichment capacity in a country could be a determining factor as to the approach to weapons material acquisition. The extent to which there is an expansion of the number of countries currently possessing reprocessing or enrichment technology associated with an expansion of the nuclear industry, there is an expansion of the potential for proliferation. However, the costs and difficulties of developing such a capability outside of the nuclear power program are not extremely large.

A subnational terrorist group is likely to be more limited in its resources, and more oriented towards diversion or theft of material. With the further development of nuclear power, the opportunity for such diversion is increased, and so therefore is the opportunity for proliferation.

The impact of the development of nuclear power worldwide affects the potential for increased proliferation in three ways:

(1) The opportunities for diversion of materials by subnational groups could be enhanced significantly. Without sufficient control on plutonium (from recycle fuel or breeder fuel) or highly enriched uranium (from HTGR fuel), there could be a significant impact on the potential for weapons proliferation.

(2) A commercial nuclear program could provide a low profile approach into weapons acquisition by providing the "cover" for the construction of enrichment or reprocessing facilities which could be used for the production of weapons materials. Because such facilities could also be constructed independently of a commercial program and supplied with fuel from either a power reactor program or research reactor program, the incremental effect on the potential for proliferation may be relatively small. It is important to assure that the utilization of such commercial facilities for weapons production be made unattractive, on balance — at least as unattractive as the construction of facilities solely dedicated to weapons material recovery.

(3) The expansion of the nuclear industry will continue to increase the availability of technology required to produce weapons material from both the reprocessing route and the enrichment route.

B. Nuclear Power Reactors/Fuel Cycles

(1) *Light Water Reactors*

As long as light water reactor fuel is enriched only to 2-4 percent, there are no opportunities for the direct use of fresh light water reactor fuel for weapons purposes. However, if plutonium is separated from irradiated fuel, there is an opportunity for the acquisition of weapons materials. Once reprocessing facilities are in place, such facilities can be used for production of weapons material or, unless security and safeguards preclude it, provide an opportunity for the diversion of plutonium for weapons use. If plutonium fabrication facilities are separate from the reprocessing site, there may be an additional opportunity for the theft or diversion of material in transit. If plutonium is not separated from spent fuel, or if plutonium is not separated from uranium, (or if the plutonium is contained in fresh recycle fuel assemblies, as in coprocessing proposals), additional separation outside of the normal commercial nuclear fuel cycle facilities would be required to recover the plutonium in a form suitable for weapons use.

The utilization of commercial uranium enrichment plants for weapons production is not possible without some modifications to these facilities. Modifications to gaseous diffusion and nozzle separation facilities would be costly and time consuming, while modifications to centrifuge or laser separation facilities might be accomplished in a relatively short period of time at relatively low cost.

The construction and operation of uranium enrichment facilities and their impact on proliferation depends largely on the type of facilities being used. Uranium enrichment processes are broadly categorized by the amount of enrichment and quantity of material handled at each enrichment stage:

(a) "High throughput, sequential low enrichment per stage": This description characterizes gaseous diffusion plants and nozzle enrichment plants. The importance of these characteristics is that once such a plant is built to produce a given level of enrichment, it is extremely costly and time consuming to modify it to produce weapon-grade materials. Thus, to the extent that light water reactor fuel enrichment programs are carried forward using such facilities, there should be no significant impact on proliferation potential.

(b) "Low throughput, parallel high enrichment per stage": This description characterizes gas centrifuge and laser enrichment plants. In such plants, there may be an opportunity, at relatively low cost, to modify output from low enrichment to weapon-grade enrichment. Thus, the degree to which such plants are built worldwide could affect the potential for proliferation. The use of such plants for weapons production would most likely be carried out by the owning nation and may be only marginally more attractive than other routes to direct production available outside the commercial nuclear program.

(2) *Breeder Reactors*

Breeder reactor fuel cycle differs from the light water reactor fuel cycle in two important respects: (a) reprocessing is not optional, and (b) fresh breeder reactor fuel offers a target for diversion since in its unirradiated state it represents a source of weapons material with relatively straightforward and low-cost chemical treatment. Since reprocessing is not optional, and plutonium must be recovered, security and safeguards must be designed to prevent national utilization of the reprocessing facility as a weapons production facility, and subnational diversion of materials. This is complicated by the fact that fresh breeder reactor fuel will in most cases be transported from plutonium fuel fabrication facilities to the power plant, thus further exposing the front end of this fuel cycle to diversion risks.

C. The Relation of Breeder Reactors and the Plutonium Economy to Proliferation

The relationship of breeder reactors and the use of plutonium to non-proliferation is a special case of the general issue of the relationship of nuclear power to proliferation. Many of the factors involved in this relationship have been discussed in Chapter II of this report. The special attention which has been focused on the breeder derives from two factors: (1) the fact that the breeder of greatest promise and most advanced state of development is the plutonium-fueled, liquid metal cooled breeder, entailing the use, production and separation of plutonium, and (2) the fact that the potential of breeders for the extension of nuclear fuel as an energy source, and for contributing to reduced energy dependence, makes them a difficult option to relinquish. In recognition of these facts, recent US policy statements have expressed continued long-term US interest in the successful development of breeder technology while placing new emphasis on the search for alternatives to the plutonium breeder which may entail less proliferation risk.

D. Accessibility of Plutonium

Separated, unirradiated plutonium is present in the system in some form from the product discharge point of a reprocessing plant, to the time of its insertion in a reactor. There are, however, considerable differences in the accessibility of this material from the viewpoint of its possible diversion for unauthorized use.

Plutonium nitrate solution and plutonium oxide prior to blending are the materials whose conversion to components capable of supporting some degree of nuclear explosion requires the least further treatment. Published works have asserted that a nuclear explosion can be sustained with high purity plutonium oxide of the type employed in breeder reactor fuel elements. The conversion of plutonium nitrate into oxide can be accomplished by the simplest form of treatment (drying and calcining), although the operation would have a high potential for dispersion of plutonium dust and would have to be conducted with at least some precautions against this hazard.

Following blending of the oxides of plutonium and uranium, the accessibility of plutonium is further diminished. It would now have to be separated chemically from the uranium oxide with which it has been blended. This requires a chemical operation which can be performed in laboratory facilities of modest size, and easy concealment. One additional complication to the potential diversion of the mixed oxides is that the quantity required has been increased considerably by dilution. The further fabrication of mixed oxide pellets into fuel pins and the combination of these pins into fuel assemblies has a further complicating effect on the physical handling of the diverted material, its visibility, and the ease of detection of a loss. However, the disassembly of fuel in these forms to allow extraction of their active material adds no appreciable new difficulty to an already highly complicated task.

The construction of a relatively efficient, high powered nuclear explosive may require plutonium metal. The conversion of plutonium oxide to metal is not beyond the capabilities of properly qualified individuals, working alone, employing small scale and relatively conventional chemical laboratory equipment. However, it does involve knowledge and skills which must be regarded as sophisticated, and which would be unlikely to be possessed even by the same individual capable of designing the explosive device. Similarly, the operations involved in fabricating plutonium into the proper forms for an explosive device, as well as those involved in the preparation and assembly of the high explosive components, involve still other backgrounds and skills, as well as, in the latter case, a high element of immediate risk. The implication of these facts is that the possibility of successful achievement of these operations by a single individual is unlikely in the extreme. The same would be true for a small group in a hurry. In a realistic view, the transformation of plutonium from any of the forms in which it exists in the breeder reactor fuel cycle into even a crude nuclear explosive is the work, not of an individual, but of at least a handful of individuals possessing different and exceptionally uncommon skills and specialized knowledge.

E. Co-Location of Fuel Cycle Operations

There is a growing interest in the possibility that the fuel cycle operations comprising reprocessing, conversion of plutonium to oxide form, preparation of mixed oxide pellets, and their fabrication into complex fuel assemblies could be performed in a single location to minimize access of unauthorized individuals to material in the forms most easily converted to explosives, and to facilitate safeguards as well as physical security.

Co-location provides some protection against terrorist diversion, but this added protection is not significantly different in degree from the protection which can be obtained through appropriate packaging and shipment procedures. The obstacles which fuel element disassembly and chemical separation of the oxides present to a national effort are insignificant. However, co-location offers major opportunities for the control of unirradiated fissionable materials inventories at the national level.

An obvious corollary of this conclusion is that the sensitive co-located fuel cycle facilities must be in locations and under control regimes which reduce the proliferation risks of these facilities to acceptable levels. The reduction through centralization and co-location in the total number of facilities at which inventories of fissionable material are held is an advantage in itself.

F. Potential Constraints on the Diversion of Nuclear Fuel Cycle Facilities and Materials for Weapons Use

The constraints to be developed should focus on the two routes to weapons materials acquisition:

- direct production,
- diversion.

In dealing with direct production, the approach should take cognizance of the fact that there are alternate routes outside of the commercial fuel cycle to weapons material production. Thus, the commercial fuel cycle route should remain at least as costly, technically and politically difficult, and time-consuming as the non-commercial route.

In dealing with diversion, the approach should take cognizance of the fact that this route is likely to be favored by subnational groups who are less likely to be technically sophisticated and more likely to accept high levels of risk. To the extent that diversion can be made both technically difficult and readily detectable, the incentive and opportunity for subnational diversion will be diminished.

(1) *Technical and Economic Constraints*

The development of technical and economic constraints on the production or diversion of weapons materials from reprocessing facilities is clarified by two questions:

- Should there be reprocessing?
- What should the reprocessing plant product be?

These questions must be evaluated together, since the benefits gained from the products of reprocessing must be sufficient to offset the costs if it is to be economically justifiable. Thus, the first question may be answered: If there is a net positive benefit to reprocessing with an acceptable product, nations will want to proceed with reprocessing.

Concerning the second question, proposals have been made which include co-processing, dilution of plutonium after separation, and spiking of plutonium with a non-fissile highly radioactive isotope such as Cobalt-60. The advantage of all of these approaches is that they produce a product which requires further processing if separation of plutonium in a form useful for weapons production is to be accomplished. Such technical approaches affect the ability of subnational groups to use such material, should a successful diversion occur.

Another more remote proposal, the tandem fuel cycle, is for spent light water reactor fuel to be further irradiated in heavy water reactors to extract available energy from plutonium and thus diminish the incentive for reprocessing.

The ability to secure enrichment facilities (particularly centrifuge or laser) in a technical manner against diversion for production use may be more difficult. An approach which may be workable would be to compartmentalize such facilities to impede the ability to convert to weapons material production.

The nozzle method is currently under development in South Africa and Germany. It may be commercially impractical for nations lacking low-cost power. Centrifuge plants may be sufficiently economic in small sizes for many nations to find them commercially attractive. Under such circumstances, they may be vulnerable to clandestine diversion.

The US, the USSR and France, among others, are actively developing laser isotope separation (LIS) technology.[1] LIS may be economic on a very small scale, making it attractive to nations with small nuclear programs. LIS

---

[1]As well, France announced in mid-1977 development of a potentially more proliferation-resistant process.

will not be feasible for even advanced countries until the late 1980s or early 1990s, and then only if a number of very difficult problems are solved. However, it is too early to forecast, at least on the basis of information in the public domain, whether this technology will be able to produce significant quantities of weapon-grade material.

(2) *Legal Constraints*

Increasingly, states have relied upon the presence of legal obligations to reduce the likelihood of diversion from a nuclear power or research project to nuclear weapons development. The conduct of US policy in this regard is illustrative of this tendency. Since the inception in 1954 of its program of cooperation for peace-time uses, the US relied upon a series of bilateral agreements with recipient states to formalize each state's commitment to non-proliferation objectives. Following the creation of the International Atomic Energy Agency in 1957, trilateral safeguards agreements were negotiated between the supplier state, the recipient state and the IAEA to provide for application of Agency safeguards to supplied materials and facilities. In the late 1960s, the need for more extensive safeguards arrangements was recognized in the Non-Proliferation Treaty which authorized the IAEA to negotiate arrangements with individual nations and regional organizations for the application of IAEA safeguards to all peaceful nuclear activities in a non-nuclear weapon state. As a result, the IAEA today is involved in administering different safeguards systems as defined in bilateral and trilateral NPT and non-NPT arrangements.

The existing framework of bilateral and multilateral arrangements is a significant factor in deterrence today. The effect of these legal arrangements in the face of other strong pressures against a state developing nuclear weapons could be enhanced, for example, by the inclusion of an effective sanctions mechanism. Both multilateral treaties such as the Non-Proliferation Treaty, and bilateral supplier-recipient agreements for cooperation in the civilian uses of atomic energy fail to specify the consequences of breach in terms reflective of the seriousness of such a breach. In the IAEA statute, the Agency is authorized to terminate safeguards, suspend membership privileges and obligations of the offending state, and report the incident to the United Nations for further action. The supplier state can reserve other rights if a recipient state breaches its safeguards obligations such as the right to recall the materials and equipment supplied. The means of enforcement of these measures, however, remain uncertain. As demonstrated by the different approaches to India in 1974 and to South Africa in 1977, it is not clear from the legal arrangements what the response of nations will be to proliferation problems.

In the course of trade under existing agreements, inadequacies in these arrangements have been identified. Under the non-NPT type of safeguards only specified facilities and materials are covered by safeguards. Until all non-nuclear weapon states not party to the NPT have accepted full-scope safeguards, they could develop a nuclear weapons potential without breach of obligations.

Many of these problems can be alleviated by amendment of existing agreements. Indeed, more recent agreements have begun to address these deficiencies. For example, the German-Brazilian agreement does require physical security measures to be applied by Brazil to the exported facilities and provides for joint German-Brazilian review of the adequacy of these measures. In the case of multilateral treaties such as the NPT, however, the prospect of modification faces considerable obstacles.

In addition to reliance on the traditional forms of legal arrangements including formal treaties and other agreements, supplier states have taken less formal measures, such as the "Zangger Committee" list, and established the London Nuclear Suppliers' Group. Developed by an international group of specialists led by Dr. Claude Zangger, the "Zangger Committee" list is of products whose supply would trigger safeguards under the NPT. The list, which includes materials and components as well as complete reactors, is intended to provide practical guidance to NPT supplier states. Periodically, supplier states continue to discuss the adequacy of existing trade arrangements to secure non-proliferation goals and to propose revision of the terms of critical provisions such as those relating to safeguards.

The Suppliers' Group Guidelines of January 1978 specify certain minimal conditions to be applied by all members to nuclear exports of materials, facilities and technology. Among the more significant of the requirements imposed by the guidelines are the applications of IAEA safeguards to all exports (but not to all peaceful nuclear activities in the recipient state), physical security measures and applications of export restrictions to facilities using technology derived from exports.

The publication of the guidelines, discussed briefly earlier, is considered notable since it is a public showing of unity by the members of the group on the need for certain restrictions on trade — although the guidelines are not as strict as those sought and unilaterally implemented by certain members such as the US. On the issue of reprocessing, enrichment and heavy water technology and facility exports, the guidelines call for members using "restraint" in making such transfers, but do not prohibit nor discourage such sensitive exports in the manner expressed by certain national nuclear export policies such as that of the US.

The London Nuclear Suppliers' Group represents an *ad hoc* extension of the NPT by its use of intergovernmental arrangements to further non-proliferation objectives. In contrast to the flow of obligations directly between weapon and non-weapon states under the NPT and bilateral agreements, the influence of the understanding achieved at the Conference on the likelihood of diversion is indirect in its implications for recipient states.

Principles governing the nuclear suppliers' guidelines include:
- Provisions for the application of IAEA safeguards on exports of material, equipment and technology;

- Prohibitions against using assistance for any nuclear explosions including those for "peaceful purposes";
- Requirements for physical security measures on nuclear equipment and materials;
- Application of "restraint" in the transfer of sensitive technologies (such as enrichment and reprocessing);
- Encouragement of multinational regional facilities for reprocessing and enrichment; and
- Special conditions governing the use or retransfer of sensitive material, equipment and technology.

These guidelines are presented *in extenso* in Volume II, Appendix D.

Necessarily, such guidelines and agreements gain force only when supported by economic and political reality. The network of existing arrangements does not sufficiently apprise recipient states of the consequences of diversion. It has been said that India accurately perceived the minimal economic and political costs of its nuclear explosion in 1974. As a new consensus emerges among supplier states, it can be expected that existing arrangements will be renegotiated to reflect the strength of the suppliers' resolve with respect to weapons non-proliferation.

In the US, both the President and Congress agree on the need to re-negotiate all existing agreements for cooperation to include tighter non-proliferation controls, e.g., required NPT-type IAEA safeguards — safeguards on all peaceful nuclear activities in a state, and required approval from the US for any reprocessing of either US-origin material or material produced through US nuclear exports. Provisions such as these are intended to close existing loopholes. This program of renegotiation is now confirmed by the passage of a legislative mandate.

Although the current US-initiated international nuclear fuel cycle evaluation (INFCE) can be expected to provide a unique forum for an exchange of views among supplier states as well as between supplier and recipient states, the INFCE participants are not committed to agreement on any set of conclusions or recommendations for action at the end of this *ad hoc* evaluation. It is not clear, therefore, what (if any) international agreements or institutions will result from INFCE.

During the period of legislated renegotiation of the existing agreements and its participation in INFCE, the US has taken interim measures including "special" legal agreements. Most prominent of these efforts is the agreement between the US and Japan for the reprocessing of US-origin material in the Tokai Mura facility in Japan, in the context of a joint program for development of safeguards and proliferation-resistant technology, with the accompanying understanding of no plutonium recycle in light water reactors, thereby both minimizing and limiting the role of plutonium.

(3) *Military and Security Constraints*

The expansion of nuclear power worldwide will significantly increase opportunities for subnational diversion of weapons materials from nuclear power programs unless security surrounding repositories for separated plutonium is at least equivalent to the security surrounding military weapons components and materials. Unless that is the criterion, there is an incremental risk that a group which is motivated to acquire a nuclear weapons capability will opt to divert material from a commercial facility. If nations are now satisfied that security at military facilities has proven to be adequate, then this level could be sufficient for commercial facilities as well. Security provisions have been developed to prevent diversion from military facilities and transportation systems, and similar systems can be developed for commercial facilities. The combination of a very high level of security and a technically complex product as suggested above should provide an adequate deterrent to diversion of such material.

VI. INSTITUTIONAL INNOVATIONS AND NON-PROLIFERATION

Other sections of this report demonstrate that the knowledge, technical capacity, and basic materials for making nuclear explosives are by now quite widespread in the world. International cooperation is therefore indispensable to any policies aimed at non-proliferation (or, more accurately, aimed at minimizing the extent and delaying the timing of any further proliferation). Such policies must seek to influence potential proliferators in two respects: reducing their *motivation* for securing nuclear weapons, and impeding their access to *means* for doing so.

Any practical set of policies will have to include some constraints and some affirmative cooperation. The broad policy orientation will probably be a judicious mix of the historical reliance on denial and sanctions organized by the "haves" against the "have-nots", and the newly evolving reliance on a proliferation-resistant regime organized cooperatively among all nations with a serious and responsible interest in nuclear power development.

From 1954 to 1974, the central principle of non-proliferation policy led by the United States and reflected in the Atomic Energy Act of 1954, the creation of the IAEA, and the negotiation of the NPT, has been based on the second of these alternatives. In effect, it has offered international cooperation in peaceful nuclear development, mainly for electric power supply, in return for a forswearing of weapons acquisition and acceptance by non-weapon states of international safeguards. Since 1974, a combination of circumstances has raised questions concerning the efficacy of those policies, leading some opinion leaders to oppose further nuclear power development in any form and others to advocate a shift towards stringent unilateral or supplier-group denials and sanctions.

This report reaffirms the utility of the earlier policy orientation, but looks to new forms of international cooperation, including institutional innovations, as the most promising means of strengthening its effectiveness in limiting proliferation. There is no realistic prospect that nuclear power will be abandoned as an energy supply option in a large number of industrial countries and a growing number of semi-industrialized developing countries. Even if it were abandoned, the dangers of nuclear proliferation would remain.

Institutional innovations are not a substitute for, but rather follow from, the basic political conviction that nuclear proliferation is a serious danger to international peace and stability, whose avoidance contributes to national security and is worth some sacrifice of national autonomy. Unless that conviction is shared by most actual and prospective participants in peaceful nuclear development, there is probably no basis for successful institutional innovation.

There is strong evidence, however, that a political consensus opposing proliferation is in fact very widely shared among both industrial and developing non-weapon states. Institutional arrangements can reinforce that consensus in four ways: (a) by improving the security and economy of fuel supply and the access to the benefits of technological improvements as they are developed; (b) by minimizing the degree of discrimination among different classes of countries; (c) by reducing the motivation for weapons acquisition arising from regional rivalries, the desire to pre-empt suspicious neighbors, or supposed prestige; and (d) by reducing the access to means for proliferation through appropriate multinational control.

In the spectrum of existing international organizations, the IAEA already has some unique characteristics, notably in the authority granted to its international corps of inspectors. Nevertheless, it remains in essence an intergovernmental regulatory agency, implementing an agreed system of safeguards over a network of national facilities. What is contemplated here goes further: transferring to multinational organizations some of the operating responsibility for portions of the nuclear fuel supply systems. Operational responsibility, in turn, requires an ability to apply factors of technical and economic efficiency more typical of industrial business corporations than of regulatory agencies.

The concept of multinational operating responsibility is flexible in two dimensions: (a) scope, and (b) degree. Scope is further discussed in the following section of this chapter. Flexibility in degree is illustrated and discussed in sections B, C, and D of this chapter.

To achieve their central objective, institutional innovations must respect both political criteria and technical/economic criteria, sometimes accepting compromise trade-offs where those sets of criteria are in conflict. For example, it could be argued that national operation of sensitive facilities in states already possessing nuclear weapons cannot directly lead to proliferation, while any form of multinational operation is likely to involve some cost in efficiency. Nevertheless, the acceptance of any multinational systems by non-weapon states is almost inconceivable unless some or all of the weapon states are participants.

As a practical matter, facilities for full fuel cycle supply may burden rather than be an advantage to an embryonic national nuclear power program. Instead of deciding that developing countries must forego them, implicitly or explicity because they cannot be counted upon to resist weapon ambitions, concerned countries could concentrate on making non-indigenous alternatives attractive and national facilities a potentially wasteful course difficult to justify. Nuclear fuel and services, in this approach, would have to be competitively priced, reliable, and efficient, with some diversification in source.

In some cases, there may well be some conflict between the objectives of economy and of non-proliferation. But if proliferation is the major potential "external dis-economy" of nuclear power, and non-proliferation a major "external economy" of an effective institutional system, it is quite proper to accept some costs, which must be internalized. One of the objectives of institutional innovations must be to reduce those costs to the essential minimum.

The political problems hampering cooperation may be eased if such cooperation is embraced in a broad approach, in which consumers as well as suppliers join in an effort, based on consent and common interest, to strengthen the non-proliferation regime by international fuel cycle arrangements which both reduce proliferation risks and provide practical assurance of equitable access.

A. Factors to be Considered in Institutional Innovations

The fuel cycle operations which are of interest in considering institutional innovations are those which give rise to the prospective availability for diversion of fissile materials to illicit uses. They are: enrichment of uranium; fabrication of highly enriched (above 20 percent) uranium-235; transportation and storage of spent fuel containing highly enriched uranium-235 and/or plutonium, and/or uranium-233; reprocessing which produces highly enriched uranium-235, or plutonium-239, or uranium-233; and processing and storage of plutonium, uranium-233 and highly enriched uranium-235. These operations are in practice generally separable, and in actual practice separated. Some may be amenable to being co-located with others. Some may not be.

Fuel cycle operations which are *not* the subject of interest in considering institutional innovations are: uranium exploration, mining and milling; conversion and fabrication of low enrichment U^{235} into fuel elements, and their transportation and storage as "fresh" fuel elements.

Radioactive waste storage and management may warrant consideration as prospectively influencing institutional innovations related to non-proliferation. International or multinational cooperation on radioactive wastes may be useful in any event and could beneficially influence willingness to cooperate in the non-proliferation related "sensitive" aspects of the fuel cycle.

The matters which must be dealt with in considering institutional innovations are in many respects common to any supply-related institution. These include: planning, organizing, financing, managing, siting, designing and constructing, operating and maintaining, marketing, contracting, accounting, security, etc. Correspondingly, such institutions are subject to applicable national law and regulation and where applicable, international law, regulation and treaties.

There now exist several such national supply institutions, with supply facilities planned or in place and operating. These include the reprocessing facilities of British Nuclear Fuels Limited (UK), Cogema (France), PNC (Japan), and DWK (Federal Republic of Germany). The Barnwell plant of the Allied General Services Co. is in place in the US but cannot operate under current US standards or policy. Enrichment facilities are planned or in place and operating in the US, the UK, France, the Federal Republic of Germany, the Netherlands, Japan and South Africa.

The general purposes which are of interest in considering institutional innovations are threefold: (1) carrying out economically and safely and in a businesslike manner the necessary supply functions, (2) providing practical political, physical and technical safeguards against diversion of fissile materials and (3) by appropriate means of inspecting and auditing, assuring the world community that all is well.

Some specific purposes to be considered include:

- Minimizing the number of "sensitive" fuel cycle supply facilities throughout the world.
- Minimizing the spread of nationally controlled sensitive fuel cycle supply facilities throughout the world.
- Limiting independent national and subnational control of and access to fissile material intended for use in nuclear power generation.
- Assuring regional and/or multinational ownership and control of "sensitive" nuclear fuel cycle facilities.
- Providing for control of and access to fissile material for use in nuclear power generation by those nations and international institutions with a responsible and harmonious interest in supply, use and control of the fissile material.

Thus, the focus of institutional innovation is on the control of and access to fissile material in certain forms. It suggests "innovative" decisions on: (1) location of "sensitive" facilities, (2) the organization and control of transportation and storage systems, (3) multinational control of access to the specified fissile materials and (4) international inspection, audit and safeguards.

Such decisions are probably more political in nature than institutional. A number of institutional concepts can be postulated which may satisfy the combined requirements of supply and non-proliferation interests. The key question may be what is politically acceptable, considering the overall interests of producing and consuming nations, especially as their interests and capabilities change with time.

B. Models and Precedents for Consideration

Many of the key problems which must be addressed in considering institutional innovations have been addressed and resolved in practice. It is possible to identify existing institutions which are in the "innovative" category and which have relevance in further consideration of non-proliferation-related institutions. These include: Euratom, Urenco, SAS, Intelsat and multinationally-owned corporations, especially Royal Dutch Shell and Unilever. Each is discussed briefly as follows:

(1) *Euratom*

Created by the Treaty of Rome (1957), Euratom is one of three European

Communities[1] established between the following nine countries: Belgium, Denmark, Federal Republic of Germany, France, Ireland, Italy, Luxembourg, the Netherlands, the United Kingdom; other countries have applied for accession. As a corrolate to the ECSC and the EEC, with whom it has the same institutions, Euratom has as its main objective to create the environment necessary for the development of a strong nuclear industry which provides extensive energy resources, leads to modernization of technical processes and contributes to the prosperity of the populations; it is to establish the conditions of safety necessary to eliminate hazards to the life and health of the public and to pursue efforts to associate other countries and to cooperate with international organizations concerned with the peaceful development of nuclear energy. Euratom is to accomplish its missions by pursuing actions in several fundamental domains, such as research, industrial development, health and safety, supply of nuclear materials, and application of safeguards.

Euratom possesses unique organizational features which might lend themselves to the development of other types of multi- or international fuel cycle organizations in three ways: (1) as an institutional model with the Euratom Supply Agency, (2) with operational vehicles such as the Joint Enterprise and investment advices through Indicative Programs, concepts which explore modes of activity development, and (3) as an advanced international safeguards system.

Euratom provides an international safeguards model with three types of basic documents: the Euratom Treaty itself, the Commission Regulation No. 3227/76 concerning the application of the Euratom safeguards provisions and the Agreements with IAEA. Moreover, each nuclear facility under Euratom safeguards is subject to a document addressing particular safeguards provisions associated with the unique technical and management characteristics of that facility. Using this foundation, requirements for containment and surveillance, material measurement, and accounting and reporting (which together comprise the safeguards program) are derived. See Volume II, Appendix C for further summary information on Euratom.

(2) *Urenco*

The signing of the Treaty of Almelo in 1970 marked the birth of Urenco, a tripartite industrial uranium enrichment organization. The three Contracting Parties are the United Kingdom, the Federal Republic of Germany and the Netherlands. They have agreed to collaborate with one another, with a view to the enrichment of uranium by the gas centrifuge process and to the man-

---

[1] The other two are the European Coal and Steel Community (ECSC), and the European Economic Community (EEC).

ufacture of gas centrifuges to that end. They promote the establishment and operation of joint industrial enterprises to build plants for the enrichment of uranium by the gas centrifuge process and to operate such plants and otherwise exploit that process on a commercial basis. Each of the Contracting Parties or commercial entities nominated by it have the right to participate equally in the joint industrial enterprises of Urenco. Finally, the three countries integrate their research in order to achieve and maintain a competitive position in relation to other sources of enriched uranium.

The Urenco tripartite structure illustrates two important features which might be applied to a fuel cycle facility: (1) a functional distribution system which provides non-proliferation mechanisms, and (2) the various institutional alternatives which exist when the national and international levels of participation within the company are distinct. First, within the Urenco structure, multifaceted functions have been delegated to component suborganizations. For example, the Joint Committee is responsible for promoting nuclear weapons non-proliferation, concerning itself with safeguards, classification arrangements, security during business transactions and fuel transport, granting of licenses, etc. The Committee provides guidance on commercial, production and R&D policy matters that could create political problems; and it facilitates the proper coordination of industrial activities and political interests.

Second, Urenco applies different rules for participation at the multinational and national levels. At the multinational level, a strictly equal partnership situation prevails. In the Joint Committee, each sponsoring government has equal representation and Committee decisions must be unanimous. Similarly, the Urenco Executive Board has three-country representation, however, its decisions need not be unanimous.

At the national level, maximum freedom for structuring country participation is allowed. The units of the Urenco consortium represent all the possible combinations of cross-tie arrangements between national parties, as well as distinct commitments between the national governments. Urenco is partly funded by two governments (the UK and the Netherlands), while the FRG's participation is totally private. Thus, various status alternatives exist: private ownership, public ownership, and hybrid private-public ownership. See Volume II, Appendix C for further summary information on Urenco.

(3) *SAS*

The Scandinavian Airlines System (SAS) consortium is founded on two constituents, the SAS Concessions and the Consortium Agreement. Of the first, the respective governments have granted the three parent companies, DDL (Danish airlines), DNLL (Norwegian airlines) and AVA (Swedish airlines), Concessions which in turn form the basis for SAS. Primarily, the Concessions standardize the legal/regulatory framework of the parent companies by extending their individual rules to each other. In addition, provisions limit the activities of each company which might conflict with current or future international agreements signed by the concert of three.

Second, the Consortium Agreement defines the operating conditions for SAS. Multinational agreement places the consortium in a private venture situation to be managed according to standard business rules. It delineates general management principles and responsibilities in such areas as: third-party liability, business allocations among partners, equity contributions for capital formation, distribution of benefits, the decision-making structure (Board of Directors), and the management control procedures (Assembly of Representatives, Board of Representatives, Accounts and Audit procedures). Finally, the document identifies solutions for typical situations such as the withdrawal of parties from the consortium, liquidation, and arbitration.

The effectiveness of the SAS Consortium is characterized by three major institutional features which facilitate private/public joint international ventures:

- an organized managerial framework,
- a simple financial structure, and
- a flexible partnership arrangement.

See Volume II, Appendix C for further summary information on SAS.

(4) *Intelsat*

The development of space communications capability by the United States in the early 1960s, and the desire to establish a global operating system, led to the creation in 1964 of the International Telecommunications Satellite consortium (commonly called Intelsat). The organization has been effective in building and operating a space communications system that serves its 86 national members, though there has been important political differences and problems along the way. The experience of that organization can offer lessons for the design of international institutional structures in other areas, especially those that are concerned with high technology subjects. In particular, there may be important lessons for a multinational nuclear fuel facility that will face at least some of the same problems. "Relevance of Intelsat Experience for Organizational Structure of Multinational Nuclear Fuel Facilities," by Eugene B. Skolnikoff, is found in Volume II, Appendix C, part IV.

(5) *Multinationally Owned Corporations*

Although hundreds of so-called "multinational" firms exist, only a handful are truly internationally owned as well as having operations in a number of countries. These five are Royal Dutch/Shell (1906), Unilever (1928), Agfa-Gevaert (1964), Fokker-FVW (1970), and Dunlop Pirelli. The first two are the oldest, and the largest.

Both Royal Dutch/Shell and Unilever are Anglo-Dutch companies. The former operates on a joint subsidiary principle; the latter functions as one company.

- *Royal Dutch/Shell*

Shell is the exception to the 50-50 division that is the rule in the other four internationally owned companies, since 60 percent is owned by Royal Dutch and 40 percent by British Shell Transport and Trading Company. This 60-40 division applies to assets, interest, and dividends on the one hand, and expenditures and costs on the other, and thus maintains a balance between the two parents' shareholders. Each operating company, and the two holding companies, are owned in this same 60-40 percentage by the two parents.

The two holding companies, Shell Petroleum N.V. (Dutch) and Shell Petroleum Limited (UK), are responsible for allocating capital investment and for profits, but the Committee of Managing Directors is the decision-making body. Composed of the managing directors of the English holding company and the members of the Presidium of the Dutch holding company, the Committee controls operating companies worldwide through four service companies.

- *Unilever*

Unilever, unlike Shell, does not sell a homogeneous commodity and therefore has had to come to grips even more with the problem of how to take advantage of the benefits of central control while not losing those of local autonomy. Unilever operates in the world consumer goods market, necessitating flexibility in modifying products to meet changing demands yet cohesion if the advantages of the very large corporation are to be realized.

A 50-50 union of Unilever Limited (London) and Unilever N.V. (Rotterdam) is closely linked by identical boards of directors in the two parent firms and equalization agreements on dividends. The chairman of Limited is a vice president of N.V. and vice versa. Only *one* parent, however, owns all (or a controlling part) of the assets of each subsidiary.

Directors of each parent's board serve on the board of the other, making the two boards identical. All 24 directors are company executives with functional or regional responsibilities to N.V. or Limited. But important decisions are delegated to the three-man Special Committee, usually composed of the chairman and a vice-chairman of Limited, and the chairman of N.V.

Product Group Coordinators and Regional Committees control, coordinate, and advise the operating companies based on the Special Committee's decisions. These groups are completely integrated between the parents.

Unilever's Annual Operating Plan effectively centralized control. Each of the 500 operating companies sends a plan up to the regional and product groups, estimating sales, margins, expenses, and profits or losses for the coming year. The Central Advisory Departments provide macroeconomic forecasts, and the regional and product groups coordinate world policy. The board and central groups make decisions about increasing output of products, plant location, buying companies, competing with other firms, and how to react to possible changes in government policy.

Centralization offers several advantages to the operating companies. The parent firms make an investment and bear a risk; they confer rights to use trademarks and patent processes; and they offer a central consulting fund of knowledge and experience in the form of the Central Advisory Departments, ranging alphabetically from Accounts and Audit to Taxation and Technical.

● *Advantages and Disadvantages of Multinationally Owned Companies*

Theoretically, the advantages of a multinational merger are three:

— "Size" effect. If the merged firm size is closer to the optimum, economies of scale should be gained. The increased cash flow can also aid R&D, marketing, training, and technical services.

— "Merger" effect. In transferring technology between the two firms, the best of each can be used to advantage. Product lines, marketing, and R&D can be rationalized.

— "Multinational" effect. The merged firm has more choices for finding the least cost site and best personnel, easier access to capital and a "home" market in two countries with corresponding advantages in government procurement.

On the other hand, increased size could produce an unwieldy, inflexible bureaucracy, and a merger could cost a lot in time, lost sales during rationalization, and low employee morale. The Bath study identified several apparently favorable features of successful multinationally owned corporations:

— equal or nearly equal size of the two merging firms;
— a complementary product mix;
— similar national business environments; and possibly
— a "bread-and-butter" product in the mature part of the product cycle, so a more rigid management structure would not handicap the firm in reacting to a rapidly changing environment.

The foregoing models are thought to have a bearing on the development of multinational supply institutions linked together by multi-tier agreements at the government and business levels.

C. Further Considerations *Re* Policy Governing Institutional Innovations

Despite important, recognized non-proliferation advantages, international or multinational fuel cycle facilities have not been generally favored by governmental authorities and industrial officials, due in considerable measure to concern that international or multinational organizations are ill-suited to the initiation, planning, management and operation of complex fuel cycle activities which have proven difficult enough to undertake on a national basis. The experience of Eurochemic, a multinational group of fourteen OECD nations, is viewed by the participants themselves as confirming rather than negating this estimate. While Eurochemic's spent fuel reprocessing plant was built and successfully operated for several years, the difficulties were reportedly substantial: costs were not well controlled; the plant was not large enough to take sufficient advantage of potential economies of scale; it suffered from a lack of financial appeal and credibility; and it bound its ability to make decisions by providing each participant with a veto. In the final analysis, the participants chose to retreat completely or to proceed nationally rather than to adopt Eurochemic as the chosen mechanism for future reprocessing undertakings.

These considerations lead to the conclusion that an important criterion in the institutional design is the separation, insofar as possible, of the functions which relate to the safeguards and non-proliferation effectiveness of the regime from those which relate principally to its operational, economic, and commercial effectiveness, creating, in effect, a two-tier system. A similar conclusion has been reached and implemented by other organizations, a notable example being Urenco, discussed earlier in this chapter.

While Urenco is a useful and interesting example, it may not serve as a general model for multinational institutions engaged in fuel cycle activities. The close political ties of the participants, which are bound together in other institutions of overwhelming economic and security importance — that is, the European Communities and NATO — are an important element in the overall assurances which the institution provides its own participants as well as their partners in these institutions. While the tripartite Joint Committee has important non-proliferation responsibilities insofar as export is concerned, it does not exercise direct materials control within the facilities, relying instead on the plant forces and the materials control system of Euratom, as supplemented recently by the IAEA-NPT safeguards responsibilities.

In the more general case, considerably greater attention to the structural details of the institution, particularly with respect to its non-proliferation effectiveness, would be required. An early, and perhaps first, consideration of the utmost importance is the national composition of the institution. The basic choices are international, more or less paralleling that of the UN or the IAEA; or multinational, meaning a much smaller number of countries, selected possibly but not necessarily on a regional basis. International organizations have the advantage in theory of providing safeguards and non-proliferation assurances which, because of the global membership, might have virtually universal acceptance. An important caveat on this consideration is the need for the organization to have the requisite operational and technical proficiency, a characteristic for which international organizations are not noted. The difficulties which the IAEA experiences in the application of its safeguards are an indication of the seriousness of this problem.

A multinational organization of numerically much more limited membership may avoid some of these operational difficulties. However, its limited membership may make its assurances, however credible they may be to its own members, lacking in credibility to the world at large, or important sectors of the world community. Nations tend not to accept safeguards systems to which they are not party. The unacceptability to the Soviet Union and many other nations of Euratom safeguards as an appropriate independent non-proliferation assurance in the context of the NPT is an example of this difficulty.

This consideration has led many to conclude that an important criterion for the composition of a multinational group is the participation, at least at the "political" tier, of nations which have genuine and self-evident diversity of interest at least with respect to the important issue of non-proliferation. An organization of like-minded nations tied together in a close security relationship (as the Soviets claim to view Euratom) would not meet this test. The participation of nuclear weapon states along with other nuclear suppliers and/or (currently) consuming nations in any multinational institution created for nuclear fuel cycle purposes would seem to be a desirable criterion.

A related consideration in evaluating the composition of a multinational institution is the technical sophistication and competence of the member nations. Even if the organization is of a multi-tiered nature, with actual operating responsibilities delegated to a competent technical organization, it is unlikely that the "political" tier can effectively and credibly fulfill its oversight responsibility if it is composed wholly of members of limited technical sophistication.

Thus, one or more members of such an organization — including at least one which is not the host country — should be of recognized technical competence. For this purpose alone, inclusion of a nuclear weapon state, or a nuclear supplier state, would seem to be indicated.

Assuming an institution of appropriate composition can be assembled, the allocation of responsibilities to its two (or more) tiers is a matter of obvious importance. While the general criterion, as noted previously, is to assign non-proliferation responsibilities to the "political" tier, and operating responsibilities to the second tier, the detailed nature of these assignments is of significance. Consideration should be given to the establishment of a safeguards and physical security force, with multinational staffing at every level, responsible directly to the political tier. The short-lived safeguards inspectorate of the European Nuclear Energy Agency (ENEA), which had responsibility for the application of safeguards to ENEA projects such as Eurochemic, is a precedent for this approach.

At the same time, extension of the multinational structure to the operating organization must also be considered. The basic purpose of separation of functions — to ensure effective performance of both non-proliferation *and* operational tasks — argues that the overriding criterion for staffing the operational tier at all levels should be merit. On this basis, purely national (public or private sector) operating organizations might be acceptable and, indeed, preferable (e.g., multinational staffing could increase the risk of technology transfer). At the same time, multinational staffing in activities which are significant from the safeguards and non-proliferation standpoint could provide important additional assurances and should be considered. There is a clear relationship between the safeguards and non-proliferation effectiveness, both real and perceived, which can be built into the political tier, and the need for extending the multinational staffing pattern to the operational tier. The more effective the former, the less will be the need to compromise operational efficiency in staffing the second or lower tiers.

An additional organizational consideration of importance is the relationship between the host country and the international or multinational institution. In the most extreme form of the concept, the international or multinational institution might itself be the "host", having jurisdiction over an international enclave. There are advantages to this concept, and it may not be so lacking in achievability as to rule out any consideration.

In the more probable case, the facilities would be located on territory of a host country, with relationships between that country and the institution regulated by agreement, preferably of treaty rank — as in the case of the centrifuge consortium. This agreement would have to prescribe a number of factors of non-proliferation importance, including

• National right or limitations on rights to interfere with the import and export of nuclear material;

• The institution's right, if any, to apply physical security measures, and the relationship or its physical security and safeguards responsibilities to those of the host country;

• The rights or limitations on rights to termination of the agreement, and the disposition of material in the event of termination;

• Sanctions for violations by either party.

It is assumed, of course, that a fuel cycle activity would, under any circumstances, be subject to the safeguards of the IAEA. The relationship between the host country, the IAEA, and the institution (if other than the IAEA) would also have to be the subject of agreement.

The operational difficulties attendant on the multinational conduct of spent fuel storage are clearly less serious than for other back-end fuel cycle operations, providing a basis for the view that spent fuel storage may offer an attractive route for the establishment and demonstration of international or multinational institutions with high non-proliferation effectiveness. At the same time, because of the possibility that such institutions, if successful, may at an appropriate later date undertake other and more complex fuel cycle activities, there is a strong incentive to design any completely new institutions initially with this flexibility in mind.

D. Some Options for Institutional Innovations

Options which may merit consideration include:
— International Cooperative with Regional Affiliates
— Multinational Fuel Cycle Centers
— Multinational Enclaves
— International Fuel Cycle Authority

These are discussed below.

1. *International Cooperative with Regional Affiliates (including presently existing facilities)*

Consideration could be given to forging an industrial consortium or cooperative suitable for the purpose of international fissile material supply and control out of certain existing, planned and future sensitive nuclear fuel cycle facilities. These might, at the outset, include Barnwell, Windscale, La Hague, Eurochemic, Tokai-Mura, Gorleben and the planned Japanese second reprocessing plant. (The United Reprocessors Group — BNFL, Cogema and DWK — could represent an interesting point of departure in considering a larger and all encompassing industrially oriented venture such as that suggested above.) Additional reprocessing capacity could be provided at existing facilities or elsewhere, as appropriate. Ownership of the industry could be shared by those contributing capital in the form of existing facilities or additional investment as it becomes required. The directors would be appointed by the share capital owners who could be from the public or private sector as national preferences dictated. The management of the corporation as a whole would be elected by the directors. The management and staffing of the operation of the individual elements would be appropriate to the location of the individual elements, i.e., generally indigenous safeguards and related non-proliferation controls would be under the supervision and subject to inspection (separately) by the international management, the board of directors, and the IAEA. Provision would be made for broadening the international scope of the corporation including capital, sites, facilities, directors, management, and operations as demand and market configuration indicated. Such provision could accommodate the interests of nations such as Brazil, Spain, Iran, etc. as they develop.

Importantly, development of this option, or some variant thereof, could enhance the prospect of having additional facilities, as they may be required, added to a pre-existing multinational cooperative of recognized value and strength, considering both fuel supply and non-proliferation. By so committing the facilities of the curent nuclear weapon states and suppliers to broad cooperative action, it could eliminate the discrimination inherent in the politically difficult premise that multinational or regional facilities are necessary only for the developing or less-developed countries. As well, it could markedly influence, in a practical and acceptable manner, the perception of need and timing of additional facilities throughout the world. Finally, this option is not necessarily inimical with the eventual development of options (2) and (3) which follow.

2. *Multinational Fuel Cycle Centers (MNFCC)*

Under this concept, a number of states would join together to form a multinational entity at a site carefully chosen with both technical and non-proliferation considerations in mind. The states concerned would agree in advance on the organizational structure of the MNFCC and the rules which would govern its actions. The organizational structure would be built up of private and public sector interests as appropriate considering both the participating states and site(s). Activities of the MNFCC might begin with spent fuel storage, which might then be followed by establishment of reprocessing and mixed-oxide fuel fabrication facilities, and waste treatment facilities once it was determined that reprocessing and recycle were needed. Reprocessing could be undertaken when sufficient fuel has been accumulated and it was clear that reprocessing was in fact desirable from the perspective of economics and resource conservation, especially for use in breeders. High-level waste disposal facilities might also be added at the same time or on an associated site.

The MNFCC concept may offer the prospect of substantial economies of scale, improved handling of storage and waste disposal, and potentially also significant advantages from the health, safety and environmental perspectives. To the extent that incentives to develop national reprocessing facilities result from a lack of adequate storage space for spent fuel, an MNFCC may help alleviate this problem by providing the necessary storage space. In this regard, centralized spent fuel storage could logically serve as a first step towards the establishment of a complete MNFCC. The transfer of spent fuel by a national participant could alleviate storage pressures in that state and, by such removal largely dispel any concern other states might have that the fuel might be diverted for military purposes. Moreover, the co-location of reprocessing, and perhaps even enrichment and fuel fabrication facilities, and the concomittant adoption of MNFCC safeguards on all fuel supplied by, as well as in the custody of, the MNFCC, could enhance both the supply security and the proliferation resistance of fuel supplies, by the simple expedient of forming an MNFCC "fuel bank".

The most important intrinsic non-proliferation advantage of the MNFCC concept is the fact that the MNFCC may offer some nations an incentive to forego the establishment of a nationally based nuclear fuel industry including reprocessing facility, due to prospectively more attractive economic, environmental, waste disposal and other features of the MNFCC. There is the possibility that an MNFCC could perform functions which certain nations cannot, or would choose not to, e.g., radioactive waste disposal.

Thus, the possibility of achieving significant practical benefits from an MNFCC may induce countries to forego or delay consideration of acquisition of national facilities. If, as appears likely, this has as its consequence a reduction in the number of national facilities constructed, non-proliferation goals would be directly served.

The full realization of the non-proliferation benefits of MNFCCs would depend in part on the details of how and where an MNFCC is established, the rules governing its actions, and how extensively it is used by the member states.

3. *Multinational Fuel Cycle Enclaves*

It may be useful to consider a variant of the MNFCC option that could have a better chance of eliciting political acceptance internationally, but would still do the job in terms of assuring nuclear fuel supplies, while having a significant limiting effect on proliferation. The variant would be the creation of multinational fuel cycle enclaves which would internationalize the territory and the control of material of dedicated "national" facilities. In other words, the enclave proposal would eliminate the frequently encountered objection to internationalizing the *operations* of sensitive facilities, by congregating national — or multinational consortia — facilities in an international territory or enclave, and internationally safeguarding the access to these facilities as well as the material flows to and from the enclave. The multilateral safeguards would as well be extended on all fuel supplied from the enclave. This option has to recommend it all of the advantages of the previously discussed multinational fuel cycle centers, without those elements which may appear to contravene the requirements of national sovereignty and national self-interest. In short this option could probably work — both from the point of view of limiting proliferation and from that of credibly assuring nuclear fuel supply — and it might just prove to be politically acceptable, as well. At the same time, it must be recognized that the limitation of national facilities to location within international enclaves, subject to international control over the inflow and outflow of materials, involves a large concession of national autonomy. Moreover, this option is perfectly compatible with the concept of multinational spent fuel storage, the logical starting point.

4. *International Fuel Cycle Authority*

A feasibility study could be made, under INFCE, of the issues involved in establishing an international fuel cycle authority responsible for the control of fissile material requiring special measures because of its proliferation potential. Issues to be examined would include: founding nations, and provision for adding nations as "owners", organization, exact scope of operations, authorities and limitations, funding, method of operating, relationship to other relevant international organizations, relationship to founding nations and their national institutions, relationship to other nations and other relevant matters. A particular emphasis of this study should be the role of international authority in controlling the disposition of material and its physical protection as contrasted with its role in management of supply operations. Past proposals for the establishment of international or multinational nuclear fuel enterprises have met with disfavor, in part because of genuine doubts as to the capability of a multinational entity for developing, building, and managing these complex facilities. Analysis of the objectives of the multinational approach indicates that the objectives should lie in the province of safeguards and physical security — not management and operations. Accordingly, it may be possible to develop arrangements which provide for genuine international jurisdiction — not simply inspection rights — over sensitive nuclear facilities and their product, including full control over its use. Financing, design, ownership and operation of the facilities could then be reserved for national, private or public companies or voluntary multinational industrial groups. In exploring this approach, innovative institutional arrangements, including the location of nationally owned facilities in international enclaves, should not be excluded.

E. Potential Limitations of Institutional Innovations

While any of these institutional arrangements might well offer very substantial advantages over a further spread of national facilities in terms of non-proliferation and the effective application of safeguards, it should also be noted that there are some potential limitations to the concept in terms of non-proliferation. Some of these are discussed below.

- *Need to maintain an equitable balance of benefits*

Unless care is taken to assure a full balance of benefits among all the parties to a multilateral institution, some states may feel that the institution is not fully meeting their needs, and that the incentives for joining are insufficient. Thus, it would be important that states participating in such an institution have a full right to capital participation, a right to some say in running the organization, a right to share from the gains of the venture, a right to have their fuel stored, and — if it comes to that further step — to have their fuel reprocessed and to obtain value from the reprocessing, and finally a right to have their firms or nations participate in share of the construction, supply of equipment, materials, etc. An equitable sharing of benefits would be in keeping with the rights and obligations of the NPT.

- *Technology Transfer*

Some concern has been expressed that technology transferred directly or inadvertently for multilateral, non-proliferation reasons might be subsequently used instead for national purposes not supportive of and possibly contrary to non-proliferation interests of other members of the institution in cases when appropriate precautions are not taken.

However, the issue of technological dissemination versus internationalization of the fuel cycle should be faced on its merits. It should be recognized that safeguards against the transfer of knowledge are far more difficult to erect than safeguards against transfer of sensitive materials or highly specialized equipment. An effort to maintain a class of technologically deprived countries would raise serious questions of conflict with Article IV of the NPT and might become a positive impetus to ambitious developing countries to overcome the discrimination.

A careful and deliberate judgment may have to be made, therefore, between the hope of gaining a few years through a policy of technological denial and the establishment of a potentially long-lasting multinational system including the most likely potential proliferators. Unless a convincing case can be made for constructive use of those "gained years" (whose number can be easily overestimated), the balance of judgment would appear to favor internationalization.

- *Takeover problem*

Hypothetically, if a nation were to become a host of a multinational facility which included a reprocessing plant and then were to seize that plant through nationalization or abrogation of the agreements with the other partners and the IAEA, it would have at its disposal a much larger quantity of material and a much larger facility than if it had established a national facility. An additional problem arises in the case of international conflict, concerning who would be responsible for securing the facility physically against outside attack.

- *Nonparticipation*

Due to the desire to develop weapon capability or for some other reason, a nation may refuse to participate in a multinational arrangement. While this in itself could arouse suspicion, the reasons given by that nation could be quite plausible in appearance and the nation might be recalcitrant without giving clear grounds for sanctions. The only recourse open to the participating nations would be denial of supply. The larger the number of such participants, the greater the difficulty in remaining outside, and the fewer the supply alternatives.

F. Opportunities and Constraints *Re* Institutional Innovations

The opportunity exists for the US, working cooperatively with the European Community and Japan and others to further develop a multinational nuclear fuel cycle supply system which is proliferation-resistant, and in which other nations participate as founders and users — and as producers when appropriate. Other nations may support such a system only if it includes the technical and economic capacities of the US and other industrialized nuclear power states and clearly provides for participation by other states in roles commensurate with their economic and energy interests and capabilities.

The opportunity for bringing about productive innovations would appear to be enhanced by: (1) beginning with, or making maximum use of existing national facilities and institutions — private and public, (2) expanding from such a base on a pragmatic and controlled basis, and (3) keeping to the necessary minimum of size and complexity the international or multinational overlay required to control, inspect and audit access to sensitive materials.

National legal requirements might cause major constraints; on the other hand, the opportunity is to establish legal rights and responsibilities which subordinate these constraints.

The problem appears to be clear, and practical solutions are at hand.

Whether and how they are applied will be a consequence of just how seriously the matter of non-proliferation is taken by the United States *and* other nations and the extent to which they care to exhibit political will and finesse in putting cooperative innovative solutions in place.

Working out of detailed arrangements for multinational operating institutions is likely to be easier than securing the political consensus for their establishment. This requires a convincing demonstration to countries in a variety of political, geographical, resource, and developmental conditions that a multinational nuclear supply system is the superior option for each of them compared with realistic alternatives — superior in terms both of reliable and economical energy supply and in terms of national security.

VII. ELEMENTS OF A NON-PROLIFERATION STRATEGY

Clearly today there are limits to the effectiveness of any non-proliferation strategy. In terms of the technology, past practices have not contained the problem, but rather have allowed it to grow to the point where today many non-weapon states have the technical capability to produce nuclear weapons. It is therefore not useful to define a non-proliferation strategy exclusively or even primarily in terms of an embargo on technology transfers.

A. Objectives of the Strategy

The capability to make nuclear weapons has become a permanent part of the world's political and technical landscape. Furthermore, a select group of six states has openly declared its possession of this power, with several other states known or surmised to have this capability. The essence of any non-proliferation policy, therefore, must be the reduction of the risk of the further spread of nuclear weapons. Even the elimination of all nuclear trade could not achieve zero risk of further proliferation. Analysis of past and present policies underscores the fundamental problem of identifying immediate and longer-range goals of a realistic future strategy. To date, states individually and collectively have failed to identify the kind of objectives which a generally acceptable non-proliferation strategy ought to pursue. Nor do we know for sure whether, in view of the continuing progress of civil nuclear technology, the traditional distinction between "nuclear weapon states" and "non-nuclear weapon states" will remain politically, militarily, and hence psychologically as relevant as it has been to date. Furthermore, modern conventional weapon technology is moving in a direction which, in terms of effectiveness, could blur more and more the time-honored distinction between "conventional" weapons and small nuclear weapons. Both weapons development and arms control have reached a point beyond which new and highly complex questions about the future of armament, its political implications, and its "controllability" (or rather non-controllability) will emerge. These developments are bound to have considerable effect on the value of nuclear weapons and the "prestige" of belonging to the "have" nations who possess them. Any sensible non-proliferation strategy, if it is to last, must address these questions.

At the outset, the problem of controlling proliferation should be thought of in a dynamic and global perspective, in view of its integral relationship to other important international questions. Hence, non-proliferation policy must be woven more closely into the fabric of foreign policy and arms control policy. Nuclear weapon states must accept the role of nuclear power as an alternative energy source. It is not furthering the control of proliferation to ban the export of nuclear power systems since the technology for its development is no longer tightly held by a select group of "have" states. Such a ban would eliminate the benefit of the current system whereby exporting nations have been able to impose safeguards as a condition to the supply of goods and services.

"Technical fixes" cannot suffice at this critical juncture. Reliance on technical approaches alone may be counter-productive over the long run if it obscures the need to reduce the political and security incentives to nuclear weapons acquisition.

The corollary objective of a non-proliferation strategy should be that of preserving the benefits of nuclear energy while fashioning effective disincentives and removing temptations for its military use, thereby reducing the risk of diversion to an acceptable level and maintaining controls (i.e., safeguards) to provide a requisite degree of assurance as to its peaceful use. Necessarily, this will involve placing non-proliferation in its proper context as an important element of international relations involved with a variety of sensitive issues. Presumably, this was the intent of the new US legislation.

It is important to avoid a narrow definition of the objectives of policy, and a narrow definition of the activities and instruments that constitute policy. The narrowest definition of "proliferation" is the acquisition or demonstration of nuclear explosives by additional national governments, or the theft or capture of nuclear weapons or their ingredients by national governments or others. The NPT endows the subject with an official definition, a discrete and irreversible one, focused on developments such as that which occurred in India. A broader definition of non-proliferation policy includes treaties, agreements, export controls, licensing arrangements and foreign aid programs that relate *directly* to nuclear energy, together with domestic nuclear policies that affect the motives and opportunities of foreign governments. Although it may be diplomatically useful to treat any particular step as a "crossing of the Rubicon", it would be a mistake to concentrate all concern and interest on that single event. It would be a similar mistake to think that "non-proliferation policies" are the only policies affecting proliferation.

As indicated by the above discussion of the fundamental premise of future non-proliferation policy, the nuclear "have" nations must direct at least some of their attention to control of the *direct* threat of nuclear proliferation posed by *their* own possession of nuclear weapons, quite apart from the relatively indirect relationship between nuclear power and weapons development and use. With this refocusing on the problem, a more realistic and acceptable strategy can take shape. A coordinated effort aimed both at limiting the deployment of existing weapons and prevention of further development of such weapons will require some sacrifices by both the nuclear "have" and "have not" nations. Each group would receive a meaningful assurance of non-proliferation without undue sacrifice of the nuclear power option.

It would exacerbate the drive toward proliferation to fail to express the goal of non-proliferation in terms of the mutual interest of nuclear weapon and non-weapon states in the success of the effort. This aspect of the issue is not recognized in present institutions such as the London Suppliers' Conference, or policies such as those contained in the unilateral statements of stricter export controls issued recently by the US and Canada. In the long run, unilateral actions by individual countries or classes of countries are stopgap in nature and will be effective only temporarily. Instead, common views and the perception of mutual interest must be developed beyond simple rhetoric and promises into joint action.

If the motivation for nuclear weapons acquisition is largely due to a perceived need for independent defensive strategy within a region, real assurances to limit proliferation can only be obtained if these defense needs are otherwise satisfied, or if it is made abundantly clear that any such employment by a nation will be counterproductive. The great determinants of nuclear weapons policy for most countries, therefore, will relate to security concerns, not controls on nuclear technology and its transmission, on the export of nuclear fuels and equipment, even on negotiated regimes for physical security and multinational surveillance. The main American policies will concern defense, the NATO Alliance, international economics and energy, troop deployments, military responses, Middle East negotiations, developing relations with China, detente with the Soviet Union, regional problems of Latin America, Africa and Asia, and the continued abstinence from the use of nuclear weapons.

This consideration of the totality of those aspects of foreign policy affecting a state's motivation to proliferate is not meant to replace the present framework which addresses the issue in specific terms related to the application of safeguards to the nuclear fuel cycle. Rather, this perspective is useful because it will provide the impetus for a continuing discussion of nuclear issues and dangers. As long as nuclear capabilities remain only "high policy", it will be hard to make an issue of something without making it a big issue. A function of "non-proliferation activity" is to allow issues to be anticipated, to deal with some of them casually and in low key, to provide assurances and reassurances, to make it hard for governments to proceed "innocently" into situations that might ultimately alarm their friends, and generally to avoid the kinds of crises that led to the French-American dispute over the Pakistani export contract or to the German-American and Brazilian-American estrangement over the Brazilian export arrangement.

B. Participants to be Considered

In contrast to past and even current policies, a future non-proliferation strategy must seek the participation of as many states as possible to ensure a solution acceptable to a wide spectrum of interests. Presently, the groups directly involved in the nuclear power controversy are polarized despite their mutual interest in the security of the world community. The following interest groups should be considered to identify the different viewpoints with respect to non-proliferation.

1. *The United States and the Soviet Union*

Since analysis of a state's motivation to go nuclear tends to confirm the presence of a fear of falling victim to an indirect confrontation between the two superpowers in regional struggles (e.g., the Middle East, the Horn of Africa) it is logical and necessary to involve these two states in a process of fashioning incentives for third nations to stay non-nuclear. There is currently no effective dialogue between these superpowers and the developing recipient states on non-proliferation policy in this broad sense.

The economic element of the relationship between superpower supplier states and recipient states has sometimes been down-played by the former. In the US, President Ford expressly stated that non-proliferation concerns, not economics, would control US domestic and export nuclear policy. President Carter has argued that the economics of the sensitive technologies, such as the plutonium breeder and reprocessing, do not support their use in the foreseeable future. The Russians have not joined the US-announced deferral of reprocessing and development of the plutonium breeder, but have announced that they will continue the planned development of an ambitious breeder program.

If the USSR and the US were to continue to oppose transfer of sensitive technologies to both NPT and non-NPT non-nuclear weapon states, limitations unique to the policies of each superpower would arise. For the US, despite its effort to achieve "consistency" between domestic and export policies in its position on reprecessing and the breeder, its supplier role will continue to shrink as recipient states find other suppliers or begin indigenous programs rather than peg their energy policy to the US which, as yet, has not developed the means for an assured fuel supply on reasonable economic terms.

2. *Other Supplier States*

Despite the independence of their conduct in recent years, other supplier states have indicated very recently their deference to the position which the US and the USSR seem to be approaching. As the US nuclear export policy entered into a phase of reconsideration after the Indian explosion of 1974, states seeking nuclear equipment and materials were offered a variety of other sources including the United Kingdom, Canada, France and West Germany. There was competition among vendors in terms of price and substance. Thus, France and West Germany entered into transactions with non-NPT states which included transfer of reprocessing technology and facilities. Canada, France and West Germany entered into contracts to sell nuclear equipment and material to developing countries which heretofore had been considered politically too unstable to provide the necessary non-proliferation assurances. For these supplier states, however, the economics of the nuclear trade was a significant factor affecting nuclear export policy. Furthermore, each supplier required acceptance of safeguards which equalled or surpassed those ordinarily required in non-NPT states on exports.

The acceptance by France and West Germany to reconsider their export policies affirms the influence of the US and the USSR in the non-proliferation policy-making process. Canada's stricter export policies, as announced in December 1976, represent the most stringent limitations imposed by any supplier state to date.

Earlier in 1976, Canada had announced its decision not to resume nuclear trade with India, with whom it has not engaged in such trade since the 1974 explosion. India's refusal to accept the safeguards required by Canada deadlocked negotiation of a new agreement for nuclear cooperation. A similar refusal by Pakistan in 1976 to agree to further safeguards led to Canada's refusal to supply nuclear fuel to that nation for which contracts had already been negotiated.

It is not clear yet how Australia will implement its announced intention to begin exporting uranium. It is expected to impose conditions on exported material akin to those adopted by Canada. In this regard, it has been suggested that joint or parallel nuclear export policies will be followed by Canada, Australia and the United States as the principal suppliers of uranium in today's market.

Despite their apparent agreement with the US as to the need for further non-proliferation controls on the transfer of sensitive nuclear technologies, there are substantial differences between the position of the US and most other supplier states, with the exception of Canada and perhaps Australia. Whereas the US and Canada have an abundance of uranium reserves and alternative energy sources, European supplier states do not have a viable energy alternative to nuclear power other than imports, and even then they must rely on imported uranium.[1] A policy of limiting their own domestic nuclear programs to power reactors, without any other fuel service facilities, and most particularly those for breeders, is unattractive if not indeed unacceptable. For these supplier states to cooperate in the US program, therefore, would require their submission to an unjustified degree of dependence on US domestic and export policies. Moreover, it would require these states to participate in an embargo of those very services upon which they must rely for their future energy supply. The embargo could involve breach of existing agreements by the supplier states, which they have expressly refused to do (e.g., the position of Germany in the transaction with Brazil, and that of France in the contract with Pakistan). Their sensitivity to the validity of existing agreements is understandable since they must rely in dealings with the superpowers on the validity of the negotiated agreement, not on a threat of arms or on technological superiority. The position of the European supplier states, weapon or non-weapon, must therefore be viewed from their domestic and international perspective. The complete nuclear fuel cycle is an important and integral part of their domestic energy policies whose value they cannot discount in a non-proliferation policy. Moreover, they cannot dispute the binding effect on existing legal arrangements without thereby also weakening their position vis-a-vis the superpowers as defined in existing agreements.

---

[1]W. Robert Keagy (Switzerland) comments: Not quite, it is a question of cost and desire, e.g., the extensive shale deposits in Sweden. Also land ownership rights in most of Europe do not admit exploration for and development of mineral deposits.

3. *Third World Recipient States*

Presumably, the greatest threat of proliferation can be traced to those recipient states which face the greatest insecurities in terms of regional defense, energy supply, economics, internal political instability and even survival. They are sometimes referred to as if they were an homogeneous mass of developing third world states with unstable governments and over-ambitious plans for development. This characterization is only helpful, however, in explaining the response of some developing states to the non-proliferation issue as but a further instance of that brand of paternalism practiced by industrialized states, led by the US and the USSR, which is offensive to their sovereignty. This interpretation of the "non-proliferation issue" is fortified by the nature of the remedy offered — elimination of the nuclear power option altogether or the embargo of fuel cycle facilities. This solution, when unmatched by any equally effective collective effort to control nuclear arms already in existence, once again illustrates the distrust of developed states that so often prevails in developing countries and the assumption that developing countries *must* trust in the nuclear weapon states not to use nuclear weapons. If this trust is intended to run only one way, it thereby creates further motivation for dependent, developing countries to upset the *status quo* of the nuclear weapon states in order to obtain access to the peaceful benefits of nuclear power — otherwise denied to them despite all non-proliferation guarantees they may be willing to give.

Supplier states, by their monopoly of nuclear technology, have thus far been able to dictate conditions in the transactions with recipient states that go beyond the economic, including assurances of non-proliferation and acceptance of effective safeguards. When this monopoly disintegrates, there is no institutional framework to replace it which would provide a meeting place for the weapon and non-weapon nuclear states to discuss their mutual problems. Non-delivery of reactors to such states, therefore, rather than delivery of them with IAEA safeguards, may create the greater risk of proliferation. The chasm between supplier and recipient states was dramatically illustrated by the disputes which emerged during the IAEA's 1976 annual meeting in Rio de Janeiro. Recipient states voiced concern that the Agency was not responsive to their needs for technical assistance in the peaceful use of nuclear power. Rather, they charged that the Agency's attention has been unduly directed to the safeguards aspect of the non-proliferation issue which concerned mostly supplier nuclear weapon states. For these recipient states, the primary problem remains energy supply.

It is the individual circumstances of each developing state which determine whether it will develop nuclear weapons. The developments in India and the rumored efforts of such countries as Pakistan and Israel demonstrate the need for an individual analysis rather than generalizations or technical fixes that might apply accross the board. The efforts, known or suspected, of such states could be explained in terms of regional defense problems aggravated by a deficiency in the alliance network or other arrangements that might provide them a degree of security they do not have now.

Within this group of recipient states, as within the group of industrialized non-nuclear weapon states, the most recent embargo announced by the US, and echoed to a more limited extent by other supplier states, has led to questioning among developing and developed non-nuclear weapon states alike as to the validity of the NPT as a continuing element of non-proliferation policy. As emphasized by non-nuclear weapon states, such as Japan and West Germany, the attraction of the NPT was its promise to cooperative action in sharing the benefits of nuclear power for peaceful purposes, without limitation to current uranium reactors, in the framework of complete IAEA safeguards and prohibition of explosives and military usage.

4. *Interrelationship Between Groups in the Nuclear Market*

The formulation of a policy specifically addressed to control weapons proliferation while using peaceful nuclear power is impeded by the myriad of interests — economic and political — which clash within and between groups. On the suppliers side, an initial period of minimal cooperation after the signing of the NPT in 1970 was gradually replaced by a competitive market in which suppliers defined divergent export policies.

More importantly, the development programs of the supplier states diverged to the extent that states assigned differing priorities to different routes toward commercialization of the full fuel cycle. To an extent, this pattern has been temporarily interrupted as each supplier state pauses to reconsider the structure of the future nuclear market. They must now decide whether fuel cycle service centers should be exported as national facilities or maintained under international or multilateral auspices.

C. Sanctions

The deterrent power of sanctions — both multilateral and unilateral — warrants serious attention and analysis in formulating future non-proliferation policy. What are needed are internationally agreed criteria and a spectrum of appropriate and credible responses relative to the seriousness of the perceived threat.

The purpose of sanctions is three-fold: to dissuade potential proliferators, to prevent the erosion of safeguards effectiveness, and to reinforce international political norms against proliferation.

Any sanctions strategy should permit some degree of flexibility. This can be accomplished by a strategy of combining two postures: one threatening automatic imposition of sanctions where a clear violation of a legal obligation is involved; a second designed to create a strong presumption that sanctions might be imposed even following more ambiguous violations. Because there may be such ambiguous violations as well as clear-cut cases, the possibility of graduated sanctions in the nuclear field may be contemplated.

A list of potential sanctions might include:

- Termination of some or all forms of nuclear cooperation
- Delaying or withholding of economic assistance
- Delaying or blocking of access to Export-Import Bank and World Bank loans
- Imposition of a multilateral trade embargo
- Refusal to continue supplying conventional arms and associated military training assistance.
- Withdrawal of a prior security guarantee
- A ban on private investment within the country in question
- Expulsion of a country's science and engineering students, termination of landing rights for its airline, prohibition of tourism to and from it, and severance of communications and representation
- Expulsion from the IAEA
- Private (commercial) sanctions, such as not extending bank credits, blocking assets, etc.

D. Policy Options

Any strategy addressing non-proliferation will necessarily be a mixture of many elements: technical, political, economic, military, paramilitary, and institutional. The policy options relate to the relative emphasis assigned to each of these areas.

1. *No Technical "Fix"—But Some Technical Help*

Technical options are limited in view of the degree to which the technology required for proliferation has already spread beyond the supplier states; yet there remain significant steps of a technical nature which can be taken. Safeguards have provided a valuable degree of assurance and should be continued, preferably by the IAEA rather than by individual states. Continued reliance upon safeguards and the IAEA, however, will require development of safeguards suited to a wider variety and number of facilities than currently under IAEA safeguards. The feasibility of a satellite system to provide additional surveillance should be considered in this regard.

A delay in the export of enrichment and plutonium separation facilities is only a temporary measure. It has been emphasized, however, as an effective deterrent to automatic acceptance of the plutonium economy. Supplier states are investigating "proliferation-resistant" fuel cycle technology as a partial technical solution to the problem. Examples of research in this regard have included review of the tandem fuel cycle, the thorium fuel cycle, co-precipitation in order not to separate plutonium alone, and "spiking" fuel with highly radioactive elements. A committee has been formed within

INFCE to evaluate these technologies. But a purely technical approach cannot alone come to grips with an ever more complex process in terms of technology and the number of states involved.

What is at issue is not simply the question of whether sensitive activities, such as plutonium recycle and accumulation, can take place with adequate assurance against proliferation, but whether any peaceful nuclear activities can proceed without unacceptable proliferation risks. Given the accessibility of reprocessing technology and the ability of even moderately industrialized nations to build workable reprocessing facilities, a diversion of spent fuel undertaken by a nation possessing only reactors will have the same consequences as a diversion of separated plutonium. The difference in time will be dependent on whether the reprocessing facility was built in advance, before the diversion occurred. A decline in confidence in the effectiveness of sanctions could well lead to a breakdown in the restraints which exist presently to deter the violation of peaceful undertakings. What is needed is a conscious and systematic cooperative effort to create an overwhelming presumption that material violations of non-proliferation undertakings will be dealt with swiftly and severely.

2. *Certainty of Specific Sanctions* vs. *General Consultative Responses*

Another policy option to be considered in deriving a more effective sanctions system is whether efforts should be made to reach prior international agreement on specific sanctions, or whether emphasis should be placed on consultative mechanisms and agreements in principle to take severe action, without specifying the level of severity. Although the certainty of specific sanctions is a desirable approach to the problem, it has distinct limitations:

• the difficulty of foreseeing in advance the wide variety of circumstances and potential remedial measures which might surround specific violations,

• the lack of credibility, even in light of treaty undertakings, that specific harsh sanctions will, in fact, be implemented.

In the preceding section we have examined policy options as they relate to the existing international sanctions mechanisms and the possibility of rigorous supply denial. The discussion to this point has dealt with these sanctions as they might be applied to nations which have violated specific non-proliferation engagements. It has been suggested additionally that penalties should be imposed on *any* nation which acquires nuclear weapons, regardless of whether it has undertaken not to do so. Yet it may not be possible to achieve broad international agreement on sanctions against the acquisition of nuclear weapons where there is no violation of any agreements, especially as the nuclear weapon states retain their own capabilities.

The supplier states, in particular the US and USSR, have the ability to fashion political, economic and military incentives and disincentives for non-weapon states in furtherance of non-proliferation. Security assurances and promotion of regional security agreements could be included in a comprehensive policy.

3. *Codes of Conduct*

The "sanctions problem" is therefore the perceived need for internationally agreed criteria and a spectrum of appropriate and credible responses that are assured, apparent and effective, and not dependent upon *ad hoc* joint or collective collaboration. This need is filled in part by the NPT; but that formal treaty mechanism, triggered by complicated international IAEA inspection and accountability procedures, lacks both speed and flexibility.

An approach that could complement the NPT/IAEA procedures would be an international instrument of moral, political and economic suasion, a code of conduct with broad and open membership. Such an instrument in the nuclear field, with widespread international support, could serve as the rapid and flexible early warning and response system that would complement the more technical and legalistic IAEA procedures, and, ultimately, the UN Security Council as final resort.

While an international code of conduct would clearly be inadequate standing alone, if it were combined with the NPT on one hand, and the Suppliers' Guidelines on the other, they could reinforce each other and in combination serve as a proliferation-resistant institutional web, at least forestalling flagrant abuses.

4. *The Ultimate Sanction*

The future development of an international sanctions system is made possible largely as a result of one fortuitous fact: as it turns out, key countries which do not yet possess nuclear weapons capability are those countries which, in advancing stages of development, are projected to have a high dependence upon nuclear energy to supply their future economic needs. In other words, at a reasonably sophisticated stage of economic — and therefore of technological — development, the chances of seeking a nuclear weapons option are inversely proportionate to the degree of energy independence. That this is the case — for whatever reason — means quite simply that the "ultimate sanction" in the nuclear politics of the future will be the threat of exclusion from a world nuclear energy supply system that works.

Exclusion from a world nuclear energy supply system, however, would require the enormously difficult task of forging agreement among a wide spectrum of countries to commit themselves in advance to apply sanctions to a nation which might break the rules of the non-proliferation game. Few countries are willing to undertake such commitments in advance since the violator may turn out to be an ally, or the calculation of their overall national interests for a given case may dictate against the application of sanctions. Thus there is a fundamental dilemma. Nations want to retain flexibility but truly effective sanctions require widespread cooperation and commitment.

Those countries which are reported variously to have the capability of producing nuclear weapons include South Africa, Israel, South Korea, Taiwan, Australia, Sweden, Switzerland, Japan, West Germany, Iran, Argentina, Brazil, conceivably East Germany, perhaps a few more. Most of these countries have available one of the three key factors in the production of peaceful nuclear energy: (1) natural uranium; (2) enrichment (or reprocessing) technology; or (3) reactor/generation technology. Several — South Africa, for example — have two of these key factors. But none has all three. South Africa is dependent upon external supply of light water reactors and generating systems in order to utilize its own natural uranium and its acquired enrichment technology. Israel is in a somewhat different but analogous position. And most if not all of the other "high risk" countries are at least as susceptible to supply interruptions of one or more of these three critical elements of nuclear power. Consequently, if the world nuclear energy supply system disciplines itself appropriately and provides concerted and therefore effective nuclear energy supply sanctions, a country could develop nuclear weapons capability only at the explicit cost of denying itself further development of the peaceful nuclear energy option.

Given the problems of world oil supply, and in light of the proposed concerted action by the nuclear supplier countries, only a nation with a truly independent energy supply would be able to risk acquiring and demonstrating nuclear weapons capability. Such a development could narrow the field of probable nuclear weapon countries considerably — to those nations which might conclude that short-term regional power politics outweighed long-term economic development; in other words, to those nations which perceived their immediate survival to be dependent upon imminent war.

The opposite perception is, of course, that of enhanced national security, including reasonably assured long-term economic growth, dependent in turn upon long-term energy supply. In the case of either set of perceptions, nuclear energy may be resorted to — either to fuel independent economic development, or to demonstrate regional nuclear weapon one-upmanship. The effective deterrent to seeking a nuclear weapons option is enhanced national security, including security of energy supply.

Continued dependence of recipient states on supplier states for fuel supply can only be justified if credible assurances of supply are forthcoming. Increased emphasis on regional energy planning could alleviate supply security concerns and increase the economic efficiency of nuclear power. Of particular interest and urgency today, given recent developments in US nuclear fuel policy, is the possibility of regional cooperation in the management of spent fuel.

5. *Managing Nuclear Fuel*

Even assuming that the planned expansion of the reprocessing installations at La Hague, France, and at Windscale, England, will be placed in service according to plan, a reprocessing bottleneck situation will probably occur. The present insufficient reprocessing capacity is causing nuclear energy countries to investigate the need for storage facilities for spent nuclear fuel. Conditions for storage vary from one power plant to the next. Commonly, reactor storage pools are large enough to contain the entire reactor core if it must be discharged for any reason, as well as one to three years' discharge of spent fuel. One year's discharge corresponds to 20-30 percent of the core. Beyond this, the power utilities are able to expand their storage capacity to some extent by modest investments.

If they use these possibilities, and if spent nuclear fuel in the future cannot be reprocessed, the storage pools at many nuclear power plants will be filled by the mid-1980s. The current storage facilities are therefore inadequate, particularly since present storage facilities abroad are nearly filled now (although their capacity may be increased significantly by the installation of new compact storage racks).

If the decision is made not to plan for immediate reprocessing of spent fuel, there are basically two alternatives available. One involves terminal storage of the spent fuel in a physical state in which reprocessing is impossible in the future, while the other involves storage in such a way that the spent fuel can be reprocessed at a later date. If the possibility of future reprocessing is to be retained, the problem of long-term safe storage of spent fuel will have to be solved.

Non-reprocessing offers certain advantages from the point of view of control, primarily as regards subnational diversion. For clandestine groups, it is significantly more difficult to retrieve plutonium from fuel which is not reprocessed. The risk of plutonium being used for nuclear explosives is thus much less when the plutonium is bound in spent fuel than when pure plutonium is stored.

Multinational spent fuel storage facilities would seem to be an appropriate strategy. Centralized facilities could be operative by 1985 and could be planned so that they may be built in stages, leaving open the possibility of eventually co-locating reprocessing capacity with them. Construction time, including planning and equipping, is considered to be about three to four years.

This would also necessitate the ready availability of an international spent fuel transport system, which would have to be assured as soon as possible. Many countries, including the US and the Federal Republic of Germany, plan to avoid highway transport of spent nuclear fuels. The Soviet Union ships mostly by rail at present. (Vehicles and loads are very heavy and can weigh over 100 metric tons.) Transporting by ship offers a number of safety advantages. This reasoning reinforces the rationale of regional spent fuel storage with direct access by sea.

6. *Institutional Innovations*

From 1954 to 1974, the central principle of non-proliferation policy as led by the United States was reflected in the US Atomic Energy Act of 1954, the creation of the IAEA, and the negotiation of the NPT. In effect, the policy offered international cooperation in peaceful nuclear development, mainly for electric power supply, in return for a forswearing of weapons acquisition and acceptance by non-weapon states of international safeguards. Since

1974, a combination of circumstances has raised questions concerning the efficacy of those policies.

This report reaffirms the validity of the earlier policy orientation, but looks to new forms of international and multinational cooperation, including institutional innovations, as the most promising means of strengthening its effectiveness in limiting proliferation. There is strong evidence that a political consensus opposing proliferation is in fact very widely shared among both industrial and developing non-weapon states. As discussed in Chapter VI, institutional arrangements can reinforce that consensus in four ways: (a) by improving the security and economy of fuel supply and access to the benefits of technological improvements as they are developed; (b) by minimizing the degree of discrimination among different classes of countries; (c) by reducing the motivation for weapons acquisition arising from regional rivalries, the desire to pre-empt suspicious neighbors, or supposed prestige; and (d) by reducing the access to means for proliferation through appropriate multinational control.

The general purposes which are of interest in considering institutional innovations are threefold: (1) carrying out economically and safely and in a businesslike manner the necessary supply functions; (2) providing practical political, physical and technical safeguards against diversion of fissile materials; and (3) by appropriate means of inspecting and auditing, assuring the world community that all is well.

Thus, the focus of institutional innovation is on the control of and access to fissile material in certain forms. It suggests "innovative" decisions on: (1) location of "sensitive" facilities, (2) the organization and control of transportation and storage systems, (3) multinational control of access to the specified fissile materials, and (4) international inspection, audit and safeguards.

Such decisions may be more political in nature than institutional. A number of institutional concepts can be postulated which satisfy the combined requirements of supply and non-proliferation interests. The key question may be: what is politically acceptable, considering the overall interests of supplier and consuming nations, especially as their interests and capabilities change with time.

It is possible to identify existing institutions which are in the "innovative" category and which have relevance in further consideration of non-proliferation-related institutions. These include: Euratom, Urenco, SAS, Intelsat, and multinationally owned corporations. Specific options which merit consideration include:

- An international cooperative with regional affiliates;
- Multinational fuel cycle centers; and
- Multinational enclaves.

Further study of the institutional innovations under the auspices of INFCE is also considered appropriate.

7. Bridging Non-Proliferation Policy and Arms Control

A related policy option — a comprehensive nuclear test ban — could serve as an effective bridge between non-proliferation measures and arms control. Proponents of such a step, as outlined earlier, argue that it would address four key considerations:

• The US has a treaty obligation to continue negotiations seeking "to achieve the discontinuance of all test explosions of nuclear weapons for all time." That commitment is contained within the Limited Test Ban Treaty which was signed by President Kennedy and ratified by the Senate in 1963.

• While it cannot be expected that the People's Republic of China or France would immediately alter their current posture, a comprehensive test ban would place greater pressure on them to halt their own testing and weapon development.

• A comprehensive test ban could be a strengthening and stabilizing support for quantitative agreements on nuclear arms, such as the SALT I and SALT II negotiations.

• Finally, a permanent halt to nuclear testing by the US and the Soviet Union would add significant support to the non-proliferation effort. It would be stating to the nations which have not yet entered the nuclear "club" that the time has come for a halt to the nuclear arms race.

VIII. CONCLUSIONS AND RECOMMENDATIONS

A. Conclusions *Re* the Environment Influencing Policy Decisions

The proliferation of nuclear weapons capability is a fact: six nations to date have demonstrated that capability, to a greater or lesser extent. Four of these nations acquired the capability by producing plutonium (the USSR, and UK, France and India), one by highly enriching uranium (China), and one by developing both of these techniques simultaneously (the US). To date, none have developed weapons capability from civilian nuclear power reactors or their fuel supply.

At least two additional nations are speculatively reported in the press and elsewhere to have nuclear weapons, but up to this point have not demonstrated or confirmed that capability. Five or six more currently have the knowledge, the access to the fissile material, and the industrial base required to produce weapons — if they were motivated to do so and prepared to violate international agreements and/or understandings. It has been estimated that by 1987 a further twenty nations could be in a similar position, if they took the decision now.

A decision to seek nuclear weapons, if taken by some of these 20 or 30 countries, would not have to be dependent on civilian nuclear power. The road to nuclear weapons capability could be a direct one, as it was for the current nuclear weapon states. A country faced with a serious and imminent threat to its security, to save time, might conceivably divert plutonium from a civilian power program, providing it had designed and developed a nuclear device in advance, rather than build a production reactor or enrichment capability. It would be neither technologically nor economically desirable — much less necessary — for any country that wants a weapon to build a civilian nuclear power cycle principally for that purpose.

The existence or acquisition of civilian nuclear power in a country wishing to acquire nuclear weapons capacity may reduce international ability to *detect and deter* proliferation activities in a timely fashion. (However, a civilian nuclear power program could bring with it international inspection and control which might otherwise be absent). If civilian nuclear power involves reprocessing and enrichment facilities, or accessible fissile material, in a country, then the risks of proliferation there are increased in several ways:

• The existence of commercial and civilian nuclear power under these circumstances would legitimize the existence of the industrial capability within a country to produce or separate nuclear material which could be used in a nuclear explosive device.

• The existence of sensitive facilities and their ancillary laboratories could mask proliferating activities.

• Changes in government or government policy could lead to employment of sensitive materials and facilities for purposes for which they were not originally intended.

It is for these reasons that universal full-scope safeguards have been proposed. Once full-scope safeguards are in place, these scenarios would require diversion from safeguards.

The likelihood is that civilian nuclear power will continue to expand in most of the nuclear weapon states and "nuclear-weapon-threshold" countries, and indeed worldwide. The long-term energy supply planning of the US, the Soviet Union, the European Community, Japan and many of the developing nations has been predicated on the use of nuclear power to generate electricity. Nuclear electricity from light water and other "converter" reactors now contributes significantly to the energy supply of these countries. Facilities for uranium enrichment, reprocessing and breeder reactor development are deployed in the US, the USSR, the European Community and Japan.

The US has not had effective world control over "sensitive nuclear technology" for a long time. Nor does the US have effective control over world uranium resources — either for purposes of supply or denial. There have been recurring demonstrations of the ability of others to enrich uranium and to produce plutonium. This includes a number of non-weapon states. Consequently, while the US has some ability to materially decrease the risk of nuclear proliferation, this is limited.

While there is no unilateral solution which the US can impose, neither is there a technological panacea, a "technical fix" which could be applied to enrichment, reprocessing and recycle, and to the breeder fuel cycle, to sever their potential link with proliferation. Proposed "technical fixes" noted earlier would probably not credibly prevent national appropriation of uranium enrichment facilities or plutonium stockpiles in a country which had the political will to become a nuclear weapon state.

On the other hand, it is both possible and practical to seek out technical measures which *might* make it more difficult for nations to divert nuclear materials from peaceful uses towards nuclear weapons and *would* strongly inhibit access to fissile material by *sub*national groups. Though it is not technically feasible to prevent national diversion of special nuclear material and facilities, technology can and should continue to be developed which would further reduce the possibility of theft by terrorists.

The prevention of proliferation will not be assured by unilaterally developing alternative fuel cycles or delaying reprocessing or the breeder reactor. The potential for further proliferation is both immediate and diffuse — for there are over 200 power reactors and at least as many research reactors around the world providing plutonium today. Breeder reactors are simply another potential source of plutonium, whose use requires reprocessing. Decisions concerning the use of breeders therefore determine the absolute answer as to whether or not reprocessing is necessary. In the meantime, literally hundreds of conventional reactors are in place and operating, with their attendant spent fuel problems.

B. Conclusions *Re* Policies of the United States and Other Nations

For purposes of shaping a non-proliferation strategy for the 1980s, it is useful to recognize that non-proliferation is not subject to US control and is beyond any individual nation's control. An effective non-proliferation strategy calls for unusual cooperation within the interdependent world community. If the US can forego the temptation of unilateral action, US influence and concern about proliferation can have a major effect. However, for this influence to be effective, it is important to counter supplier and recipient suspicions that the new US concern with non-proliferation — focusing upon avoidance of reprocessing and the plutonium economy — is due as much to its own economic interest as to the more important problem of world security.

In order to avoid such misunderstandings, the US should undertake to develop further and share with other nations its understanding of the nature and implications of the proliferation risks related to nuclear power, as well as learning from others their relevant views and exploring the differences. The US should also participate with others in developing a shared understanding of the nature and implications of the proliferation risks as a precursor to seeking international or multinational consensus on the technical and political measures required. The United Nations, the IAEA, the London Suppliers' Group and INFCE provide useful forums for the continued development of such understandings. Seeking a working international consensus on technical and political measures is likely to require the focused multilateral efforts available from such forums.[1]

A related difficulty is that the US Federal government remains poorly equipped to deal with important issues that combine both foreign and domestic elements. US Government agencies with foreign relations functions traditionally have little interest in, or responsibility for, what goes on at home, while those with domestic functions have relatively little interest in, or responsibility for, what goes on abroad. Energy policy and natural resources policy are beset by foreign supply considerations, domestic constituencies, and fragmentation of authority among the 50 states. The isolation of domestic from foreign affairs may have been tolerable in simpler times. Now, policies for energy, nuclear power, non-proliferation and natural resources demand integration of foreign and domestic considerations. Yet, the foreign policy establishment's position in the existing structure of government does not encourage its direct contact with US industrial suppliers and electric utilities, for example. Effective future policy for non-proliferation will require substantial innovation in organization and functioning of both the

---

[1] It is in this context that the current question of the continued existence and future form of the London Suppliers' Group meetings might usefully be examined.

executive and legislative branches of the government as well as the private sector to assure coordination of their actions in the spheres of foreign and domestic policy.

For the greatest effect, US efforts should be focused through an international dialogue with supplier and recipient states. It may still be possible for the supplier states, for a limited time, to exact assurances of non-proliferation from recipient states. However, this leverage will be short-lived. There is little time — but absolute need — for US non-proliferation policy to be coordinated with other aspects of foreign policy, and in particular with defense and economic issues. Furthermore, non-proliferation policy must attempt to provide the countries using nuclear energy with solid reasons not to receive or develop sensitive nuclear materials or facilities. Recipient states, therefore, must be consulted — and listened to — during the policy formulation process, with particular emphasis on the assurance of nuclear fuel supply security.

In order to be effective, nuclear fuel supply security would have to be both economic and credible. While US policy makers would probably be willing to pay a "non-proliferation premium", in the form of an assured economic supply internationally, the US would be binding itself to a commitment which would appear to be vulnerable to the vagaries of its political process and to competition with domestic nuclear fuel needs. A more attractive and effective alternative would be US commitment to one or more multinational nuclear fuel supply sources. The starting point in any process of internationalizing the fuel cycle could be the provision of spent fuel storage facilities. Nuclear waste management could be provided on a multinational basis as an incentive to those countries willing to place national reprocessing facilities under international control in a multinational nuclear fuel supply system.

National decisions concerning reprocessing and the breeder reactor will eventually affect the amount of high-level waste disposal and spent fuel storage needs, but cannot alter the fact that they are needed now and on an increasing scale that cannot be met by individual countries acting alone. The logical starting point is, therefore, to organize multinational facilities which can meet the spent fuel storage need, and which can evolve to meet other fuel cycle supply needs as and when those functions are incorporated in the multinational system.

The International Nuclear Fuel Cycle Evaluation (INFCE) affords the world community an unusual opportunity to explore alternative fuel cycles from the perspective of the most knowledgeable supplier and recipient states. Current non-proliferation hopes appear to rely too heavily on unproven technical approaches. Evaluation of the benefits and feasibility of these technical approaches should take place in the course of INFCE. As the evaluation allows a dialogue among supplier and user states, a record should emerge which will serve as a useful reference for all states in nuclear energy planning.

Strengthening technical impediments to non-proliferation is necessary to the overall objective of impeding proliferation of weapon-material-production capabilities. However, sensitive fuel cycle activities currently underway should be carried forward pending completion of INFCE and further development of multinational and international auspices. When and if acceptable proliferation-resistant alternative technologies can be effectively and efficiently employed, they too could be carried out under such auspices.

If action were taken to meet the perceived need of supplying spent fuel storage and/or high-level waste management, it would appear that a parallel step may be taken to meet the perceived threat of the proliferation of national enrichment and reprocessing facilities. One approach has been for the US and other existing suppliers to implement a policy to assure the provision of enrichment services at the lowest possible cost.[2] The complementary step that could provide an alternative to national reprocessing facilities is internationalizing nuclear fuel supply services as well as their control and safeguards.

The more national adherents these multinational measures gain, the greater will be their legitimacy and supply credibility — and the more difficult it will be for individual countries to remain outside this solution, retaining sensitive national facilities. The opportunity exists for the US, working cooperatively with the European Community, Japan and others, to create a multinational nuclear fuel cycle supply system in which other nations participate as founders and users — and as producers when appropriate. As envisioned, such a system would be as (or more) proliferation-resistant than the dispersed, once-through fuel cycle with indefinite spent fuel storage. Other nations may support such a system only if it includes the technical and economic capabilities of the US and other industrialized nuclear power states, and clearly provides for participation by other states in roles commensurate with their evolving economic and energy interests and capabilities.

The opportunity for bringing about productive innovations would appear to be enhanced by: (1) beginning with, or making maximum use of existing national facilities and institutions, private and public; (2) expanding from such a base on a pragmatic and controlled basis; and (3) keeping to the necessary minimum of size and complexity, and maximum of speed and effectiveness, the international system required to control, inspect and audit access to sensitive materials.

National legal requirements could cause major constraints on such innovations; on the other hand, the opportunity is to establish legal rights and responsibilities which subordinate these constraints. The problem appears to be clear, and workable solutions are at hand. Whether and how they are applied will be a consequence of the extent to which the US and other nations care to exhibit political will and finesse in putting cooperative, innovative solutions in place.

---

[2]Recommended by the Atlantic Council in its earlier report, *Nuclear Fuels Policy,* pp. 58-60.

Working out of detailed arrangements for multinational operating institutions is likely to be easier than securing the domestic and international political consensus for their establishment. This will require a convincing demonstration to countries in a variety of political, geographical, resource, and developmental conditions that a multinational nuclear supply system is the superior option for each of them compared with realistic alternatives — superior in terms of both reliable and economic energy supply and national security.

The following recommendations support the goal of meeting nuclear fuel supply requirements while optimizing safeguards against nuclear proliferation.

C. Recommendations

1. *Comprehensive Energy Policy*

As a matter of course, the United States and other industrialized countries should adopt and implement comprehensive, long-term energy policies aimed at reducing, by strict energy conservation measures and by maximum development of alternate energy sources and resources, their dependence on imported petroleum. The US could and should take the lead. This action would help to alleviate pressures on the world petroleum market, to stabilize petroleum prices, and to contribute to making the diminishing world petroleum reserves available, under acceptable conditions, to others, particularly to the less developed countries.

2. *Renegotiation of Existing US Commitments*

In implementing non-proliferation policy, the US government should first acknowledge the validity of its existing agreements for cooperation, subsequent arrangements and contracts concerning nuclear supply, and in that context, and in a spirit of partnership, proceed to negotiate further desired conditions of supply for nuclear exports.

3. *US Approach to Other Countries*

The US should tailor its approach to non-nuclear weapon states to help meet their specific needs — political and security as well as economic — so as to offset the pressures for national nuclear weapon capability. US policy should reflect the distinction between the near-term, country-specific proliferation threat of nations close to weapon capability now, and the longer-term threat of additional countries approaching the same threshold in the course of their further economic and technological development. The US should take a case-by-case approach in forestalling countries close to proliferation. For countries further from proliferation, the US approach should try to encourage them to join the US in forming a system which will preclude their need to produce sensitive nuclear materials nationally.

4. *US Nuclear Energy Assistance*

By facilitating the transfer of non-sensitive nuclear materials and technologies, the US should demonstrate that adherents to the NPT, and others accepting full-scope safeguards, can enjoy the benefits of nuclear power without possession and use of sensitive nuclear materials and technologies.

5. *Credible Free World Fuel Supply*

The US should promptly make domestic and multilateral arrangements to provide a credible assured nuclear fuel supply to states desiring to develop nuclear power which are adherents to the NPT or otherwise accept full-scope safeguards.

6. *Multinational Spent Fuel Storage*

Supplier and recipient states should jointly ensure that multinational spent nuclear fuel storage facilities are operative and adequate to meet their needs by 1985 at the latest. These facilities should be planned so that they can be built in stages, leaving open the possibility of eventually co-locating with them other fuel cycle facilities.

7. *Multinational Radioactive Waste Management*

High level radioactive waste management should be provided on a multi-national basis as an incentive to those countries willing to place national reprocessing facilities under international control in the multinational nuclear fuel supply system described in the following recommendation.

8. *Institutional Innovations*

In implementing recommendations 5, 6, and 7 above, the United States, cooperatively with other willing nations, should develop a multinational system with the following purposes: (a) carrying out economically and safely the necessary nuclear fuel supply functions; (b) providing practical political, physical and technical safeguards against diversion of fissile materials and production facilities. This action could be initiated in conjunction with or separate from INFCE. Consideration should be given to forging a multinational nuclear fuel supply system which would utilize existing national facilities as the base for creating a broadly based institution which would enhance the security of nuclear fuels supply, and which would, under international supervision, safeguard these same sensitive fuel cycle facilities and materials.

9. *Safeguarded Transport System*

The availability of an adequately safeguarded international transport system for special nuclear materials should be assured promptly by the supplier and recipient nations, with immediate emphasis on spent fuel transport.

10. *The US Breeder Program*

The US should develop and demonstrate proliferation-resistant breeder technology in regard to reactors, fuel preparation and use, storage and transportation, reprocessing and radioactive waste management. In doing so, the US should create a positive basis for close cooperation with other nations on breeders with the intent to provide strong technological as well as political leadership internationally on developing and demonstrating proliferation-resistant technology and institutions, as well as on later deployment decisions. Plutonium-fueled breeders should be included.

11. *Strengthening the IAEA*

The continued vital role of the IAEA in the application of safeguards should be assured as a fundamental element in any non-proliferation policy. In general, IAEA member states' fuel cycle facilities — including new US enrichment capacity — should be constructed and organized to permit maximum effectiveness of inspection and accountability of material flows, and improved reliability, standardization, accuracy and quality of safeguards measurements. In particular, the US should promptly implement the safeguards agreement with the IAEA which was proposed by the US more than ten years ago.

12. *Enhancing Safeguards*

The US should continue to press for effective safeguards, both domestically and internationally. Prompt attention should be directed toward the development of safeguards for the new enrichment technologies as well as for reprocessing.

13. *Comprehensive or "Full-Scope" Safeguards*

The US should continue to press for universal adherence to the Non-Proliferation Treaty. Until such time as that goal is achieved, the US should foster a common front among all nuclear supplier and recipient countries to the effect that further shipments of nuclear fuel and equipment require full-scope safeguards on all nuclear facilities, acquired or indigenous, in the recipient country.

14. *Subnational Theft and Diversion*

The US and other governments interested in the further development of nuclear power should promptly pool information, share technical and institutional measures and, where appropriate, take concerted action which can prevent the theft or diversion of sensitive nuclear materials and facilities by terrorists and other subnational groups.

15. *Sanctions*

The US should provide — both unilaterally and multilaterally through a cooperative international regime — appropriate sanctions for any nation which chooses to violate non-proliferation commitments or safeguard agreements. The cooperative international regime would consist of supply sanctions extended by suppliers' agreement embracing all nuclear facilities of countries receiving any outside assistance or supply of fuel, facilities, or know-how. The US should take the lead in creating an international agreement or code of conduct to provide flexible early-warning and response to nuclear misconduct, complementing the more formal IAEA-NPT procedures and developing further the London Nuclear Suppliers' Group Guidelines. Specifically, this new agreement could, if necessary, trigger appropriate cooperative as well as unilateral sanctions. As well, the agreement should provide a forum for arbitration of national instances and complaints of misconduct. But the primary purpose of the initiative must remain to treat national violations with the utmost speed in the most severe manner possible.

16. *The International Nuclear Fuel Cycle Evaluation*

INFCE should have as a primary goal a thorough, balanced and objective analysis of the advantages and disadvantages of each nuclear fuel cycle with reference to economics, non-proliferation and other factors. INFCE should supplement on-going national and multinational R&D programs concerning the fuel cycle. The results of these on-going activities would be a useful and timely contribution to INFCE, while preventing strategic slippage in R&D during the course of the international evaluation.

17. *Comprehensive Test Ban*

In order to enhance international acceptance of measures to reduce the likelihood and extent of nuclear proliferation, the US, the Soviet Union, and other nuclear weapon and non-nuclear weapon states should urgently establish a comprehensive nuclear weapon test ban intended to contribute in a substantial way to reducing incentives for present non-nuclear weapon states to pursue development of technology leading to a nuclear explosive capability, and to increase the credibility and acceptability of non-proliferation measures.

GLOSSARY OF ACRONYMS

ACDA	Arms Control and Disarmament Agency
BNFL	British Nuclear Fuels Limited
ECSC	European Coal and Steel Community
EEC	European Economic Community
ENEA	European Nuclear Energy Agency
Euratom	European Atomic Energy Community
Eurochemic	Multinational group of 14 OECD countries
Eurodif	European consortium for the enrichment of uranium by the gaseous diffusion method (France, Italy, Spain, Belgium, and, indirectly, Iran)
GWe	Gigawatt of electricity
HTGR	High temperature gas-cooled reactor
IAEA	International Atomic Energy Agency
INFCE	International Nuclear Fuel Cycle Evaluation
LDCs	Less developed countries
LMFBR	Liquid metal fast breeder reactor
MNFCC	Multinational fuel cycle center
MOX	Mixed oxide
MWe	Megawatt of electricity
NATO	North Atlantic Treaty Organization
NPT	Non Proliferation Treaty
NRC	Nuclear Regulatory Commission
OAPEC	Organization of Arab Petroleum Exporting Countries
OECD	Organization for Economic Cooperation and Development
OPEC	Organization of Petroleum Exporting Countries
SALT	Strategic Arms Limitation Talks
Urenco	Partnership for the enrichment of uranium by the centrifuge method (UK, W. Germany, Netherlands)
10-CFR	The US Code of Federal Regulations, Energy Series

THE ATLANTIC COUNCIL
OF THE UNITED STATES

The Atlantic Council, established seventeen years ago, seeks to promote closer mutually advantageous ties between Western Europe, North America, Japan, Australia and New Zealand. The objective is greater security and more effective harmonization of economic, monetary, energy and resource policies for the benefit of the individual in his personal, business, financial and other relations across national boundaries. These varied and complex relationships have been and will continue to be central to the major economic and political developments which affect our international integrity and domestic well-being.

In an increasingly interdependent world where "foreign" policy is ever more closely intertwined with "domestic" policies, there is a clear need for both official and private consideration of means of dealing with problems which transcend national frontiers. The Atlantic Council is a unique non-governmental, bi-partisan, tax-exempt, educational, citizens' organization. It conducts its programs to promote understanding of major international security, political and economic problems, foster informed public debate on these issues, and make substantive policy recommendations to both the Executive and Legislative branches of the US Government, as well as to the appropriate key international organizations.

The Board of Directors of the Atlantic Council is composed of some one hundred prominent leaders and experts in business, finance, labor and education, together with former senior government officials. Their names are listed on the back cover of this *Policy Paper*.

The Atlantic Council of the United States
1616 H Street, NW
Washington, DC 20006
Telephone: (202) 347-9353

RECENT PUBLICATIONS
from the Atlantic Council of the United States

"**Security in the Eastern Mediterranean: Re-thinking American Policy**", Atlantic Council's Working Group on Security. 19 pp. $1.00. April 1978.

"**The Growing Dimensions of Security**", Atlantic Council's Working Group on Security. 90 pp. $5.00. December 1977.

"**What Future for the UN? An Atlantic Dialogue**", Atlantic Council's Working Group on the United Nations. 40 pp. $2.00. November 1977.

"**Harmonizing Economic Policy: Summit Meetings and Collective Leadership**", Atlantic Council's Working Group on Economic Policy, 1977, 24 pp. Out of print.

"**Improving NATO Force Capabilities**", General John W. Vogt (Ret.) 1977, 12 pp. $1.00

"**Détente: The Continuation of Tension by Other Means**", Timothy W. Stanley, 1977, 15 pp. $1.00

"**What Is the Soviet Navy Up To?**", Vice Admiral Julien J. LeBourgeois (Ret.) 1977, 15 pp. $1.00

"**Nuclear Fuels Policy**", Atlantic Council's Nuclear Fuels Policy Working Group, 1976, 136 pp. Out of print; available in Westview edition.

"**GATT Plus**", Atlantic Council's Special Advisory Panel to the Trade Committee, 1975, 98 pp. Out of print.

"**Financing Free World Energy Supply and Use**", John E. Gray, 1975, 38 pp. Out of print.

"**Alternative Energy Sources for the United States**", Richard J. Anderson, Peter L. Hofmann and Sidney E. Rolfe, 1975, 19 pp. $1.00

"**World Energy and U.S. Leadership**", Harlan Cleveland, 1975, 21 pp. Out of print.

"**Beyond Diplomacy**", first Interim Report of the Atlantic Council's Special Committee on Intergovernmental Organization and Reorganization, 1975, 87 pp. $4.50

The above policy papers are available prepaid from the Atlantic Council, 1616 H St., NW, Washington, D.C. 20006
(202) 347-9353

"**Nuclear Fuels Policy**", Atlantic Council's Nuclear Fuels Policy Working Group. 1976, 136 pp. $5.95

"**Nuclear Fuel and American Foreign Policy**", Edward F. Wonder, 1977, 72 pp. $3.95

"**East-West Trade: Encounter and Accommodation**", Atlantic Council's Working Group on East-West Trade, 1977, 194 pp. paper $5.95; hard cover $15.00

"**The Future of the UN: A Strategy for Like-Minded Nations**", Atlantic Council's Working Group on the UN. 1977, 58 pp. $3.95

"**The International Monetary System: Progress and Prospects**", Atlantic Council's Working Group on Monetary Policy, 1977, 86 pp. $3.95

"**The U.S. and the Developing Countries**", Atlantic Council's Working Group on Development Policy, 1977, 175 pp. paper $5.95; hard cover $14.00

The six policy papers listed above may be ordered from Westview Press, 5500 Central Avenue, Boulder, Colo. 80301.
(303) 444-3541